RAIL ATLAS
OF
BRITAIN
1977

Compiled by **S. K. Baker**

Oxford Publishing Co. Oxford

Oxford Publishing Co. 1977

SBN 86093 009 2

Maps Drawn by Paul Karau

Printed by S & S Press Ltd. Abingdon
Bound by Kemp Hall Bindery Oxford

Published by
Oxford Publishing Co
8 The Roundway
Headington Oxford

INTRODUCTION

The inspiration for this atlas was two-fold; firstly a feeling of total bewilderment by 'Llans' and 'Abers' on first visiting South Wales four years ago, and secondly a wall railway map drawn by a friend, Martin Bairstow. Since then, at university, there has been steady progress in drawing the rail network throughout Great Britain. The author feels sure that this atlas as it has finally evolved will be useful to all with an interest in railways, whether professional or enthusiast. The emphasis is on the current network since it is felt that this information is not published elsewhere.

Throughout, the main aim has been to show clearly, using expanded sheets where necessary, the railways of this country, including the whole of London Transport and light railways. Passenger lines are distinguished by colour according to operating company and all freight-only lines are depicted in red. The criterion for a British Rail passenger line has been taken as at least one advertised passenger train per day in each direction. On passenger routes, to assist the traveller, single and multiple track sections, with crossing loops on single lines have been shown. Symbols are used to identify both major centres of rail freight, such as collieries and power stations, and railway installations such as locomotive depots and works. Secondary information, for example junction names and significant tunnels, with lengths if greater than one mile, has been added in areas where clarity would not be significantly affected.

The author would like to express his thanks to members of the Oxford University Railway Society and to Nigel Bird, Chris Hammond and Richard Warson in particular for help in compiling and correcting the maps. His cousin, Dr Tony McCann deserves special thanks for removing much of the tedium by computer sorting the index, as do Oxford City Libraries for providing excellent reference facilities.

Shipley, West Yorks   Stuart K. Baker

June, 1977

Publisher's Note

Although situations are constantly changing on the railways of Britain every effort has been made by the author to ensure complete accuracy of the maps in the book at the time of going to press.

We must also state that the availability of information regarding all lines and track beds in Britain is not a source of permission to walk on British Rail property or explore closed lines.

KEY TO ATLAS

		Surface	Tunnel	Tube
British Rail — Passenger	Multiple Track	————	—) — — (—	- - - - - - - -
	Single Track	+++++++	++) + + (++	
London Transport *(Line indicated by code)*	Multiple Track	C ————	C —) — — (—	C - - - - - - -
	Single Track	C +++++++	C ++) + + (++	C ++++++++
Preserved & Minor Passenger Railways	Multiple Track	═·═·═	═) ··· (═	
	Single Track	—·—·—	—) ·· (—	
Freight only lines — *(British Rail & Others)*	No Single/ Multiple Distinction	————	—) — — (—	

Advertised Passenger Station:
   Saltburn ————●————

Crossing Loop at Passenger Station:
   Newtown +++++++✕+++++++

Crossing Loop on Single Line:
   Murthly +++++++✕+++++++

Unadvertised/Excursion Station:
   Warrenby* ————●————

				LM ER
Major Power Signalboxes	PRESTON	B.R. Region Breaks		——|——
Carriage Sidings	—| C.S.	Colliery *(including opencast site)*		————▲
Freight/Marshalling Yard	TINSLEY	Power Station		————△
Freightliner Terminal	—| FLT	Oil Refinery		————●
National Carriers Depot	——| NCL	Oil Terminal		————○
Locomotive Depot/Stabling Point	■ BS	Cement Works or Terminal		————■
British Rail Engineering Ltd.	▨ BREL	Quarry		————□
Junction Names	—|— *Haughley Junc.*	Other Freight Terminal		————|

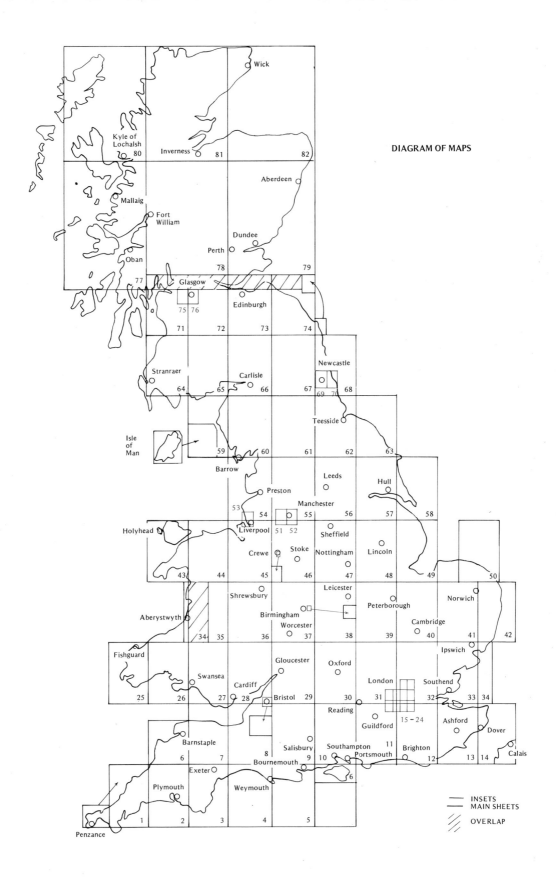

DIAGRAM OF MAPS

Wick

Kyle of
Lochalsh
80   Inverness   81   82

Mallaig

Fort
William   Aberdeen

Dundee
Perth
Oban   Glasgow
78   79
77
Edinburgh
75 76

71   72   73   74

Newcastle
Stranraer   Carlisle
64   65   66   67   69 70   68

Teesside
Isle
of
Man   59   60   61   62   63

Barrow
Leeds   Hull
Preston
Manchester
53   54   55   56   57   58
Liverpool
Holyhead   51 52   Sheffield
Crewe   Stoke   Nottingham   Lincoln
43   44   45   46   47   48   49   50

Leicester
Shrewsbury   Norwich
Birmingham   Peterborough
Aberystwyth   Cambridge
Worcester
34   35   36   37   38   39   40   41   42

Ipswich
Fishguard
Gloucester   Oxford
Swansea   London
Cardiff   Southend
25   26   27   28   Bristol   29   30   31   32   33   34

Reading
Guildford   Ashford
15 – 24   Dover
Barnstaple
Salisbury   Southampton   11
8   Portsmouth   Brighton   Calais
6   7   9   10   12   13   14
Bournemouth
Exeter
6
Plymouth   Weymouth

1   2   3   4   5

Penzance

INSETS
MAIN SHEETS
OVERLAP

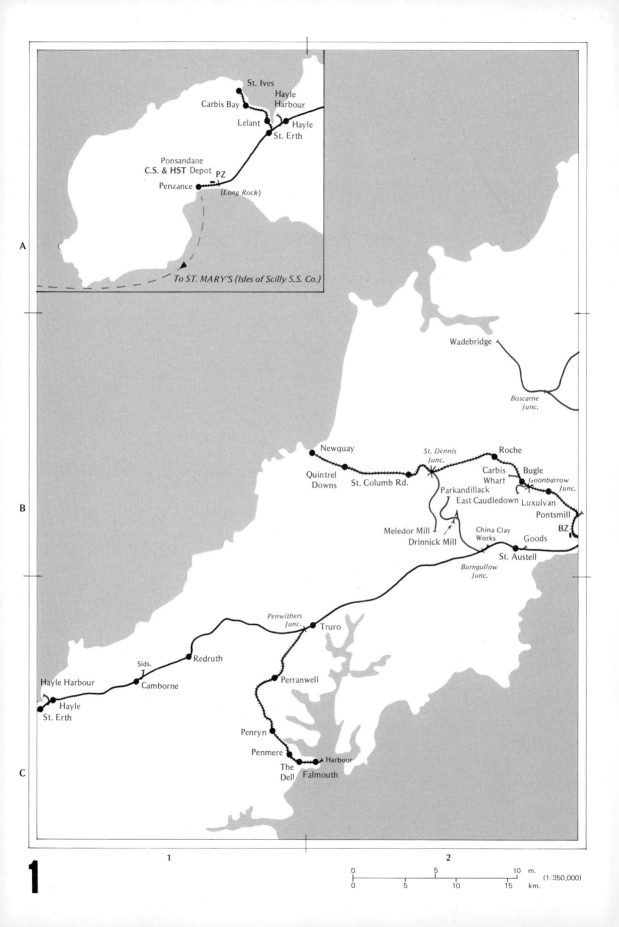

A

St. Ives
Carbis Bay
Hayle Harbour
Lelant
Hayle
St. Erth

Ponsandane
C.S. & HST Depot
PZ
Penzance
(Long Rock)

To ST. MARY'S (Isles of Scilly S.S. Co.)

Wadebridge

Boscarne Junc.

Newquay
Roche
St. Dennis Junc.
Quintrel Downs
St. Columb Rd.
Carbis Wharf
Bugle
Goonbarrow Junc.

B

Parkandillack
East Caudledown
Luxulvan
Pontsmill
Meledor Mill
China Clay Works
Drinnick Mill
Goods
BZ
St. Austell

Burngullow Junc.

Penwithers Junc.
Truro

Redruth
Perranwell
Sids.
Camborne

Hayle Harbour
Penryn
Hayle
St. Erth
Penmere
Harbour
The Dell
Falmouth

C

1

2

0   5   10   m.
0   5   10   15   km.

(1:350,000)

1

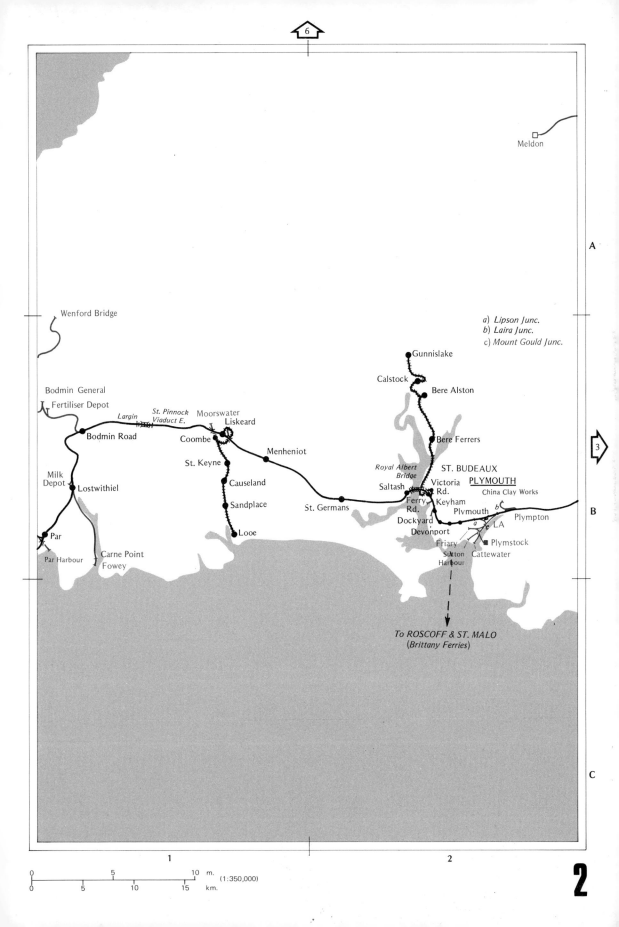

6

Meldon

A

Wenford Bridge

a) *Lipson Junc.*
b) *Laira Junc.*
c) *Mount Gould Junc.*

Gunnislake

Calstock

Bere Alston

Bodmin General

Fertiliser Depot

Largin *St. Pinnock Viaduct E.* Moorswater

Bodmin Road Coombe Liskeard

Menheniot

Bere Ferrers

St. Keyne

Royal Albert Bridge

ST. BUDEAUX

Milk Depot

Lostwithiel

Causeland

Sandplace

St. Germans

Saltash

Victoria Rd.

Keyham

PLYMOUTH

China Clay Works

3

Ferry Rd.

Plymouth

b

Plympton

B

Looe

Dockyard

Devonport

a

LA

Par

Friary

Plymstock

Carne Point

Sutton Harbour

Cattewater

Par Harbour

Fowey

To ROSCOFF & ST. MALO
(Brittany Ferries)

C

0   5   10 m.   (1:350,000)

0   5   10   15   km.

1   2

2

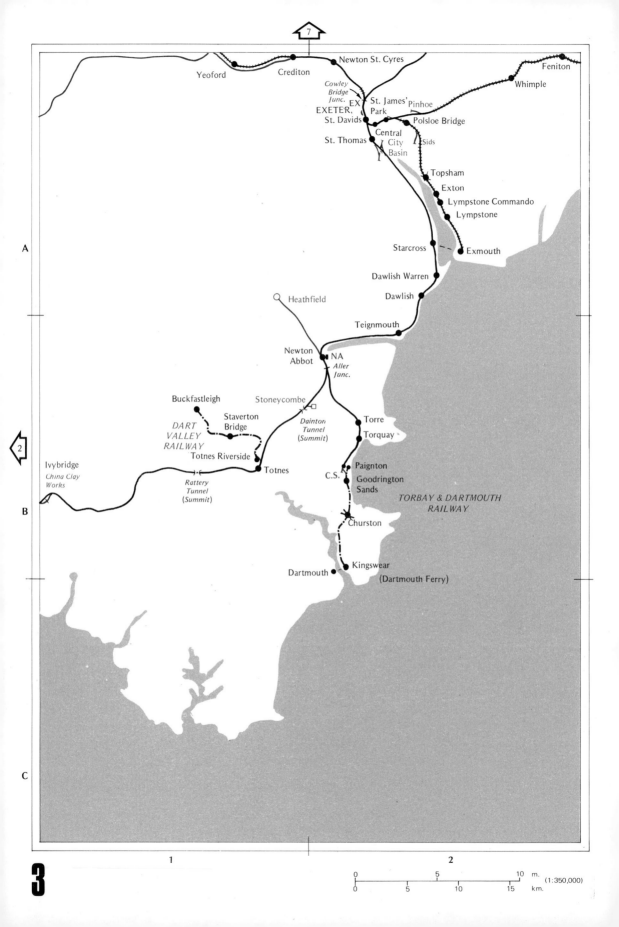

Yeoford

Crediton

Newton St. Cyres

Feniton

Whimple

Cowley Bridge Junc.

EX St. James' Park

Pinhoe

EXETER, St. Davids

Polsloe Bridge

St. Thomas

Central City Basin

Sids

Topsham

Exton

Lympstone Commando

Lympstone

Starcross

Exmouth

Dawlish Warren

Dawlish

Heathfield

Teignmouth

Newton Abbot

NA

Aller Junc.

Buckfastleigh

Stoneycombe

Torre

Torquay

Staverton Bridge

DART VALLEY RAILWAY

Dainton Tunnel (Summit)

Paignton

Totnes Riverside

Goodrington Sands

C.S.

Ivybridge

China Clay Works

Rattery Tunnel (Summit)

Totnes

TORBAY & DARTMOUTH RAILWAY

Churston

Kingswear

Dartmouth

(Dartmouth Ferry)

A

2

B

C

3

1

2

0   5   10 m. (1:350,000)

0   5   10   15 km.

Axminster

Maiden Newton

Colyton
Colyford
SEATON TRAMWAY (2' 9") Axmouth
Seaton

A

5

B

C

1
2

0   5   10 m.
0   5   10   15 km.
(1:350,000)

4

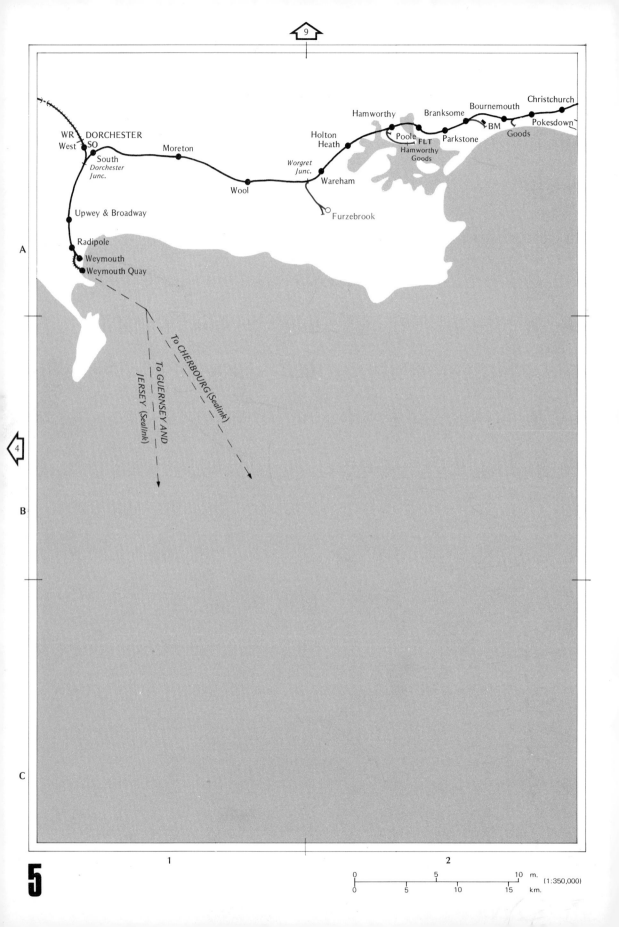

9

DORCHESTER
WR
West   SO
South
Dorchester
Junc.

Moreton

Upwey & Broadway

Radipole

Weymouth
Weymouth Quay

Wool

Worgret
Junc.

Wareham

Furzebrook

Holton
Heath

Hamworthy

Poole
Hamworthy
Goods

FLT

Parkstone

Branksome

Bournemouth
BM
Goods

Christchurch

Pokesdown

To CHERBOURG (Sealink)

To GUERNSEY AND
JERSEY (Sealink)

A

4

B

C

1

2

0   5   10 m.

0   5   10   15 km.

(1:350,000)

5

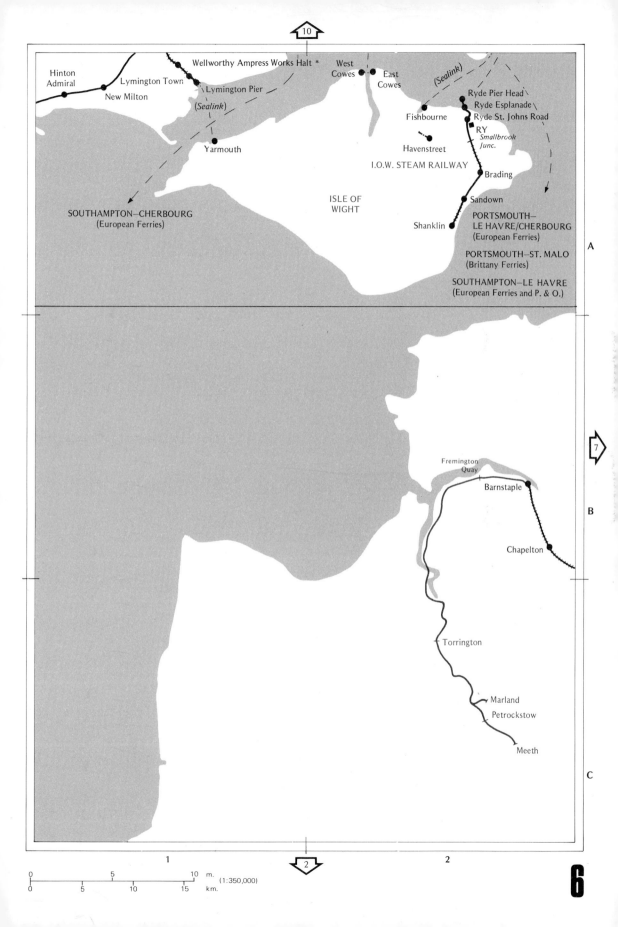

10

Hinton
Admiral

Lymington Town

New Milton

Wellworthy Ampress Works Halt *

Lymington Pier

(Sealink)

Yarmouth

SOUTHAMPTON–CHERBOURG
(European Ferries)

West
Cowes

East
Cowes

Fishbourne

Havenstreet

I.O.W. STEAM RAILWAY

ISLE OF
WIGHT

(Sealink)

Ryde Pier Head

Ryde Esplanade

Ryde St. Johns Road

RY
*Smallbrook
Junc.*

Brading

Sandown

Shanklin

PORTSMOUTH–
LE HAVRE/CHERBOURG
(European Ferries)

PORTSMOUTH–ST. MALO
(Brittany Ferries)

SOUTHAMPTON–LE HAVRE
(European Ferries and P. & O.)

A

7

Fremington
Quay

Barnstaple

Chapelton

B

Torrington

Marland
Petrockstow

Meeth

C

1

2

2

0   5   10   m.   (1:350,000)
0   5   10   15   km.

6

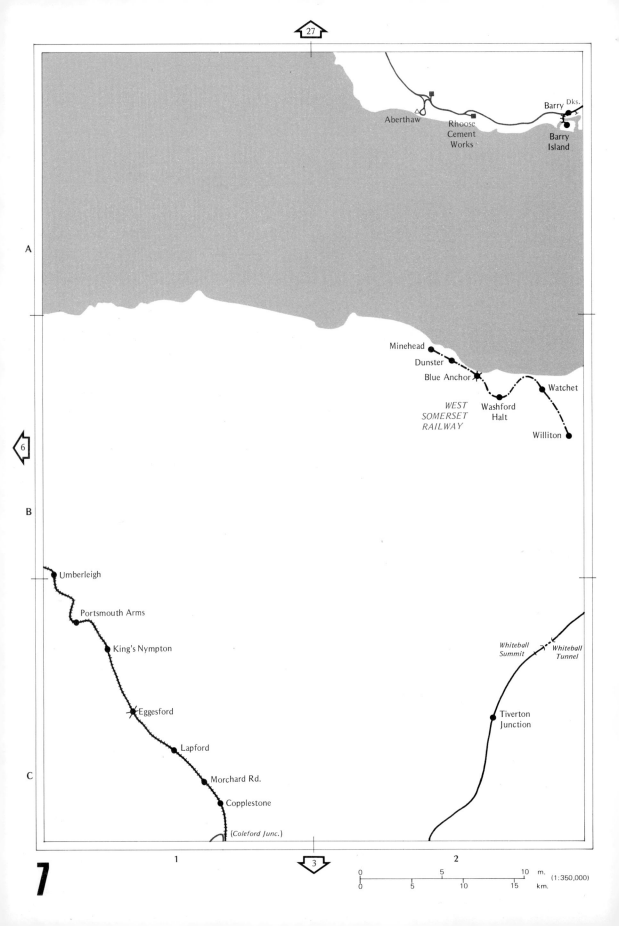

Barry ^{Dks.}

Aberthaw

Rhoose
Cement
Works

Barry
Island

A

Minehead

Dunster

Blue Anchor

Watchet

*WEST
SOMERSET
RAILWAY*

Washford
Halt

Williton

6

B

Umberleigh

Portsmouth Arms

King's Nympton

*Whiteball
Summit*

*Whiteball
Tunnel*

Eggesford

Tiverton
Junction

Lapford

Morchard Rd.

C

Copplestone

(Coleford Junc.)

7

0   5   10   m.   (1:350,000)

0   5   10   15   km.

28

Dinas
Powis
Dingle Rd.
Penarth
Cadoxton
Barry Docks
Wks.
Docks

BRISTOL
T.M.
St. Anne's
Park Tun.
Flax
Bourton
Parson St.
(SEE INSET BELOW)

Nailsea and
Backwell

Yatton

Weston
Milton
Worle Junc.

Weston-s-
Mare
Uphill
Junc.

A

Clifton Down
Tunnel
Redland
Gds.
Stapleton
Road
Montpelier
Clifton Down
Lawrence
Hill
Avonside
Wharf
Cem. T.
Wks.
Dr. Days
Bridge Junc.
a
b
Goods
Bristol
Temple
Meads
BR
PM
Whapping
Wharf
BJ
Wks.
Bristol
West Junc.
BRISTOL

Highbridge

Puriton

Ashton
Gate*
Ashton
Junc.
Bedminster

Malago Vale
C.S.
Parson Street
FLT
Ashton Gate C.S.
a) Bristol East Junc.
b) North Somerset Junc.

9

Bridgwater
Wks.

Castle Cary

B

Taunton
P.W.
Yard
Cogload Junc.
Somerton Tunnel

Sherborne
Yeovil Pen Mill
Yeovil Junc.
Thornford
Yetminster
Crewkerne
Chetnole

C

Chard Junc.
Milk
Depot
Honiton
Tunnel
Honiton

1

4

0   5   10 m.   (1:350,000)
0   5   10   15 km.

8

Keynsham

Wks.

Box Tunnel
(1 m. 1452 yds.)

Thingley
Junc.

Bathampton
Junc.

Oldfield
Park

Bath
Spa

Melksham

Bradford-on-
Avon

Freshford

e

Avoncliff

w

Bradford Juncs.

s

Pewsey

Trowbridge

Radstock

A

Hawkeridge
Junc.

Cement
Wks.

Westbury WY

Fairwood Junc.

Heywood Road Junc.

WR

Dilton Marsh

SO

Whatley Quarry
(West Somerset)

Clink Road
Junc.

Frome

Warminster

Merehead

Blatchbridge
Junc.

Cranmore

Quidhampton
Clay Term.

Tunnel
Junc.

Witham

Chilmark

WR

8

SO

Dinton

Wilton
Junc.

Bruton

B

Tisbury

Salisbury

Buckhorn
Weston
Tun.

Gillingham

Templecombe

C

9

1

5

| 0 | | | 5 | | | 10 | m. |
| 0 | 5 | | 10 | | 15 | | km. |

(1:350,000)

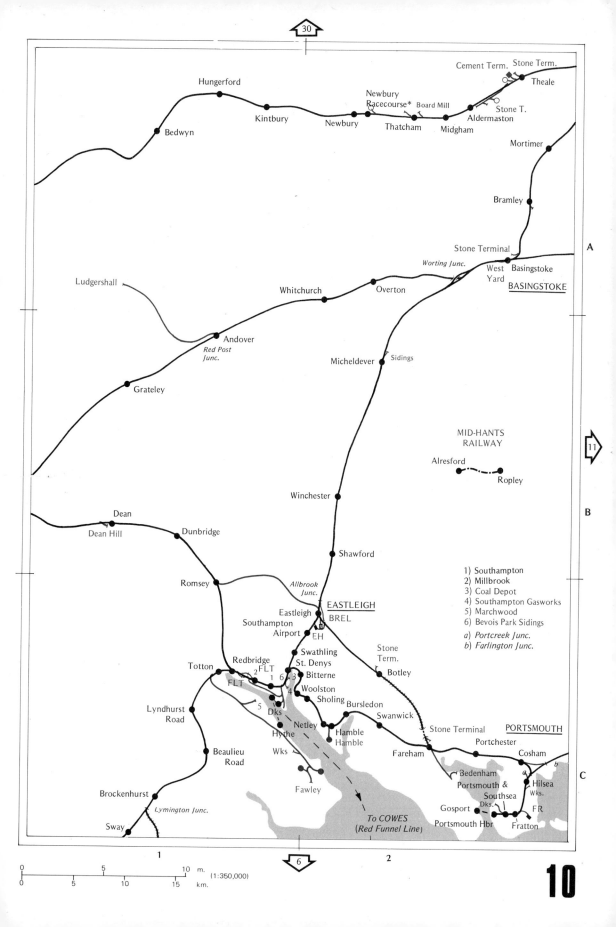

Hungerford

Bedwyn

Kintbury

Newbury

Newbury
Racecourse*   Board Mill

Thatcham

Midgham

Cement Term.   Stone Term.

Theale

Stone T.

Aldermaston

Mortimer

Bramley

Stone Terminal

Worting Junc.

West
Yard

Basingstoke

BASINGSTOKE

Ludgershall

Whitchurch

Overton

Andover
*Red Post
Junc.*

Grateley

Micheldever   Sidings

MID-HANTS
RAILWAY

Alresford

Ropley

Winchester

Dean

Dean Hill

Dunbridge

Shawford

1) Southampton
2) Millbrook
3) Coal Depot
4) Southampton Gasworks
5) Marchwood
6) Bevois Park Sidings

a) Portcreek Junc.
b) Farlington Junc.

Romsey

*Allbrook
Junc.*

EASTLEIGH

Eastleigh

Southampton
Airport

BREL

EH

Swathling

St. Denys

Bitterne

Woolston

Sholing

Stone
Term.

Botley

Totton

Redbridge

FLT

FLT

1   6   3

2

4

5   Dks

Bursledon

Swanwick

Stone Terminal

PORTSMOUTH

Portchester

Lyndhurst
Road

Netley

Hamble
Hamble

Fareham

Cosham

b

Beaulieu
Road

Hythe

Wks

Bedenham

a

Hilsea
Wks.

Brockenhurst

Fawley

Portsmouth &
Southsea

Dks.

FR

Lymington Junc.

Gosport

Fratton

Sway

Portsmouth Hbr

*To COWES
(Red Funnel Line)*

A

B

C

1

2

0   5   10 m.   (1:350,000)
0   5   10   15 km.

10

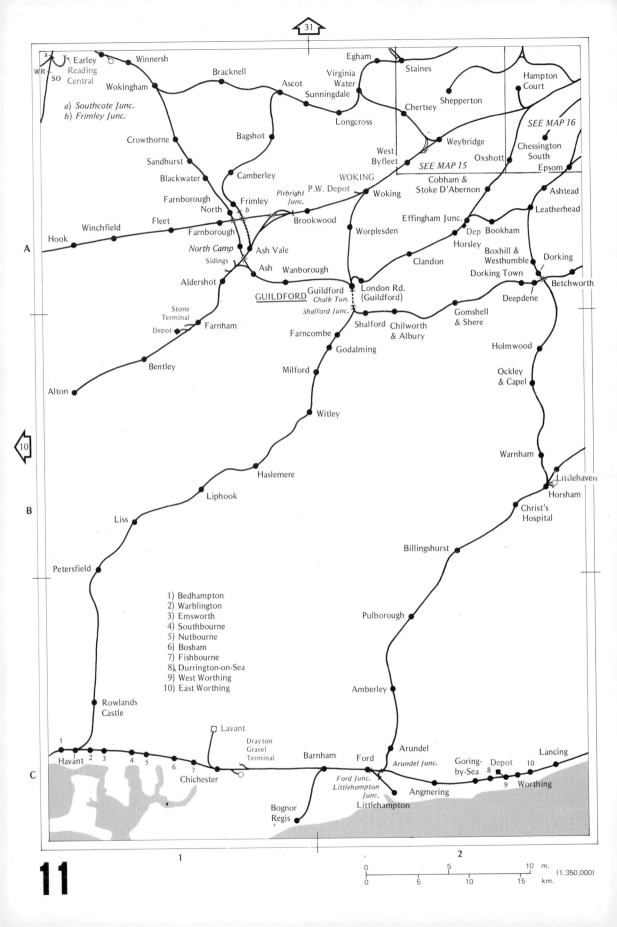

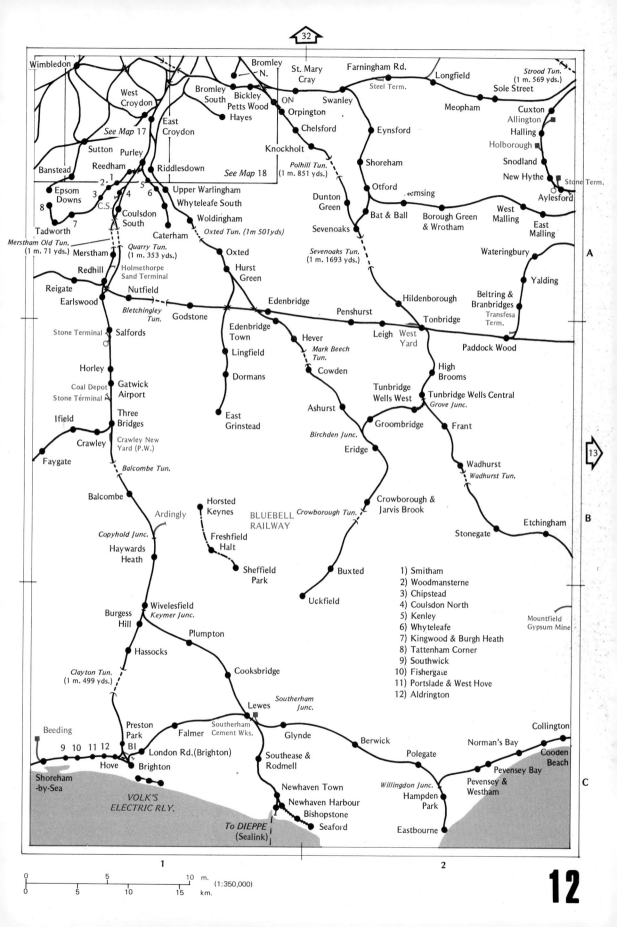

Wimbledon

West Croydon

Bromley N.
St. Mary Cray
Bromley South
Bickley
Petts Wood
Hayes
ON
Orpington
Chelsford
Farningham Rd.
Steel Term.
Longfield
Swanley
Meopham
Sole Street
Strood Tun.
(1 m. 569 yds.)

Cuxton
Allington
Halling
Holborough
Snodland
New Hythe
Stone Term.
Aylesford

See Map 17

East Croydon

Sutton
Purley
Reedham
Riddlesdown

Banstead

2-1
3
4 5 6
C.S.

Epsom Downs
8
7
Tadworth

Upper Warlingham
Whyteleafe South
Woldingham
Caterham
Coulsdon South

Merstham Old Tun.
(1 m. 71 yds.)
Merstham

Quarry Tun.
(1 m. 353 yds.)

Oxted Tun. (1m 501yds.)

See Map 18

Polhill Tun.
(1 m. 851 yds.)

Knockholt

Shoreham

Otford
eemsing

Dunton Green
Bat & Ball
Sevenoaks

Borough Green & Wrotham

West Malling
East Malling

Redhill
Reigate
Earlswood

Holmethorpe Sand Terminal

Nutfield

Bletchingley Tun.
Godstone

Oxted

Hurst Green

Edenbridge

Penshurst

Hildenborough

Tonbridge

Leigh West Yard

Paddock Wood

Wateringbury
Yalding

Beltring & Branbridges
Transfesa Term.

A

Stone Terminal
Salfords

Horley

Coal Depot
Stone Terminal

Gatwick Airport

Three Bridges

Crawley New Yard (P.W.)

Ifield
Crawley
Faygate

Edenbridge Town
Lingfield
Dormans

Hever
Mark Beech Tun.
Cowden

East Grinstead

Ashurst

Tunbridge Wells West

Groombridge

Birchden Junc.
Eridge

High Brooms
Tunbridge Wells Central
Grove Junc.

Frant

Wadhurst
Wadhurst Tun.

13

Balcombe Tun.

Balcombe

Ardingly

Copyhold Junc.

Haywards Heath

Horsted Keynes

Freshfield Halt

Sheffield Park

BLUEBELL RAILWAY

Crowborough Tun.

Crowborough & Jarvis Brook

Stonegate

Etchingham

B

Mountfield Gypsum Mine

Buxted

Uckfield

1) Smitham
2) Woodmansterne
3) Chipstead
4) Coulsdon North
5) Kenley
6) Whyteleafe
7) Kingwood & Burgh Heath
8) Tattenham Corner
9) Southwick
10) Fishergate
11) Portslade & West Hove
12) Aldrington

Burgess Hill
Wivelsfield
Keymer Junc.

Plumpton

Hassocks

Clayton Tun.
(1 m. 499 yds.)

Cooksbridge

Lewes
Southerham Junc.

Beeding
9 10 11 12

Preston Park
B1
London Rd.(Brighton)
Hove
Brighton

Falmer

Southerham Cement Wks.

Glynde

Southease & Rodmell

Berwick

Polegate

Norman's Bay

Collington

Cooden Beach

Pevensey Bay
Pevensey & Westham

Willingdon Junc.
Hampden Park

Eastbourne

C

Shoreham -by-Sea

VOLK'S ELECTRIC RLY.

Newhaven Town
Newhaven Harbour
Bishopstone
Seaford

To DIEPPE (Sealink)

1

2

0   5   10 m.
0   5   10   15 km.
(1:350,000)

12

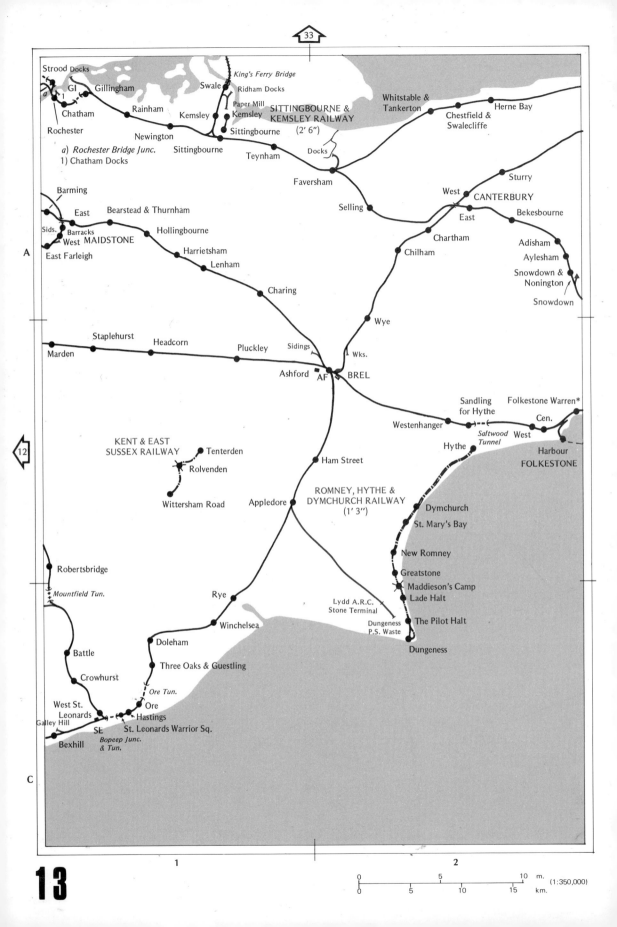

Strood Docks
a 1
Gl Gillingham
Chatham
Rochester
Rainham
Newington
Sittingbourne

Swale
Ridham Docks
King's Ferry Bridge
Paper Mill
Kemsley
Kemsley
Sittingbourne
Teynham

SITTINGBOURNE &
KEMSLEY RAILWAY
(2' 6")
Docks

Whitstable &
Tankerton
Chestfield &
Swalecliffe
Herne Bay

a) Rochester Bridge Junc.
1) Chatham Docks

Faversham
Selling
West
CANTERBURY
Sturry

Barming
East
Barracks
Sids.
West MAIDSTONE
East Farleigh
Bearstead & Thurnham
Hollingbourne
Harrietsham
Lenham
Charing

Chartham
Chilham
East
Bekesbourne
Adisham
Aylesham
Snowdown &
Nonington
Snowdown

A

Wye

Staplehurst
Headcorn
Pluckley
Sidings
Marden

Wks.
Ashford AF BREL

Sandling
for Hythe
Folkestone Warren*
Cen.
West
Westenhanger
Saltwood Tunnel
Hythe
Harbour
FOLKESTONE

12

KENT & EAST
SUSSEX RAILWAY
Tenterden
Rolvenden
Wittersham Road

Ham Street
Appledore

ROMNEY, HYTHE &
DYMCHURCH RAILWAY
(1' 3")

Dymchurch
St. Mary's Bay
New Romney
Greatstone
Maddieson's Camp
Lade Halt

Robertsbridge
Mountfield Tun.

Rye
Winchelsea

Lydd A.R.C.
Stone Terminal
Dungeness
P.S. Waste
The Pilot Halt
Dungeness

Battle
Crowhurst
West St.
Leonards
Galley Hill
SE
Bexhill
*Bopeep Junc.
& Tun.*
Doleham
Three Oaks & Guestling
Ore Tun.
Ore
Hastings
St. Leonards Warrior Sq.

C

1
2

0   5   10   m.
0   5   10   15   km.
(1:350,000)

13

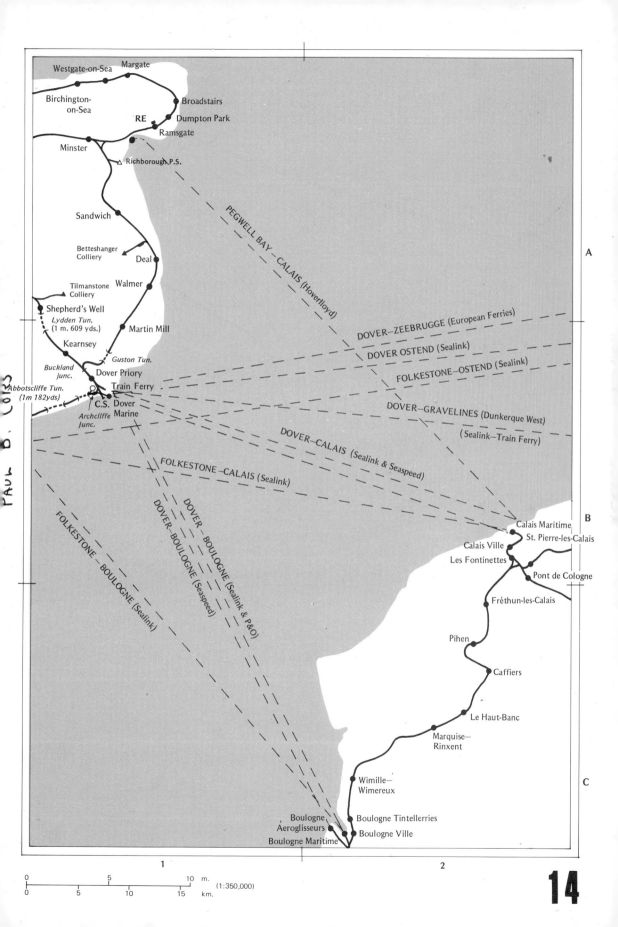

Westgate-on-Sea
Margate
Birchington-on-Sea
Broadstairs
RE
Dumpton Park
Ramsgate
Minster
△ Richborough P.S.
Sandwich
Betteshanger Colliery
Deal
Tilmanstone Colliery
Walmer
Shepherd's Well
Lydden Tun.
(1 m. 609 yds.)
Martin Mill
Kearnsey
Guston Tun.
Buckland junc.
Dover Priory
Abbotscliffe Tun.
(1m 182yds)
Train Ferry
C.S. Dover
Marine
Archcliffe Junc.

PAUL B. COLS

PEGWELL BAY – CALAIS (Hoverlloyd)

DOVER – ZEEBRUGGE (European Ferries)

DOVER OSTEND (Sealink)

FOLKESTONE – OSTEND (Sealink)

DOVER – GRAVELINES (Dunkerque West)

(Sealink–Train Ferry)

DOVER – CALAIS (Sealink & Seaspeed)

FOLKESTONE –CALAIS (Sealink)

FOLKESTONE – BOULOGNE (Sealink)

DOVER–BOULOGNE (Seaspeed)

DOVER – BOULOGNE (Sealink & P&O)

Calais Maritime
St. Pierre-les-Calais
Calais Ville
Les Fontinettes
Pont de Cologne
Fréthun-les-Calais
Pihen
Caffiers
Le Haut-Banc
Marquise–Rinxent
Wimille–Wimereux
Boulogne Aeroglisseurs
Boulogne Tintellerries
Boulogne Ville
Boulogne Maritime

A

B

C

1

2

0   5   10 m.
0   5   10   15 km.
(1:350,000)

14

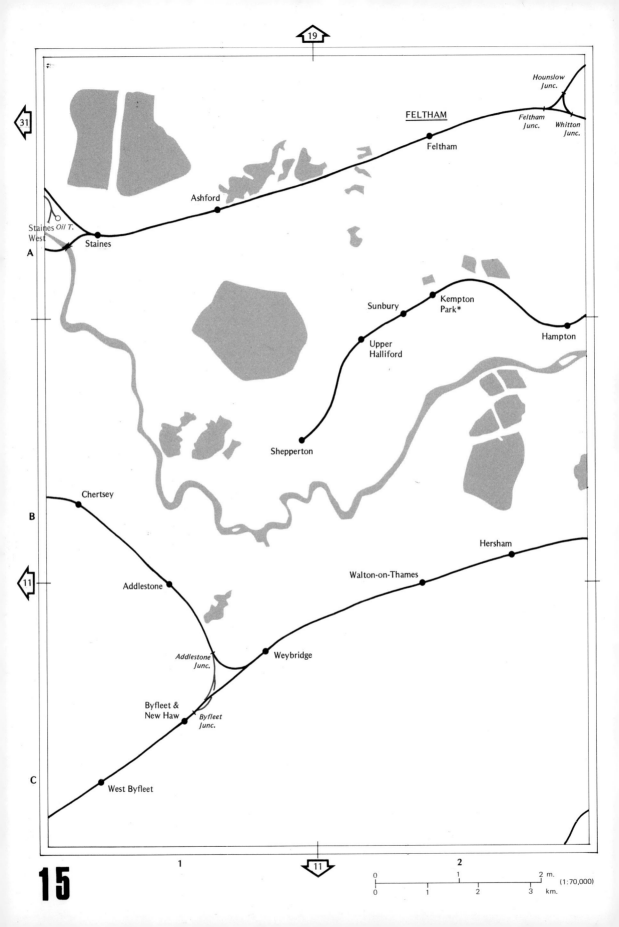

19

31

FELTHAM

Hounslow
Junc.

Feltham
Junc.

Whitton
Junc.

Feltham

Ashford

Staines *Oil T.*
West

Staines

A

Sunbury

Kempton
Park*

Upper
Halliford

Hampton

Shepperton

Chertsey

Hersham

B

Walton-on-Thames

11

Addlestone

Addlestone
Junc.

Weybridge

Byfleet &
New Haw

Byfleet
Junc.

C

West Byfleet

1

2

11

0   1   2 m.

0   1   2   3 km.

(1:70,000)

15

St. Margaret's

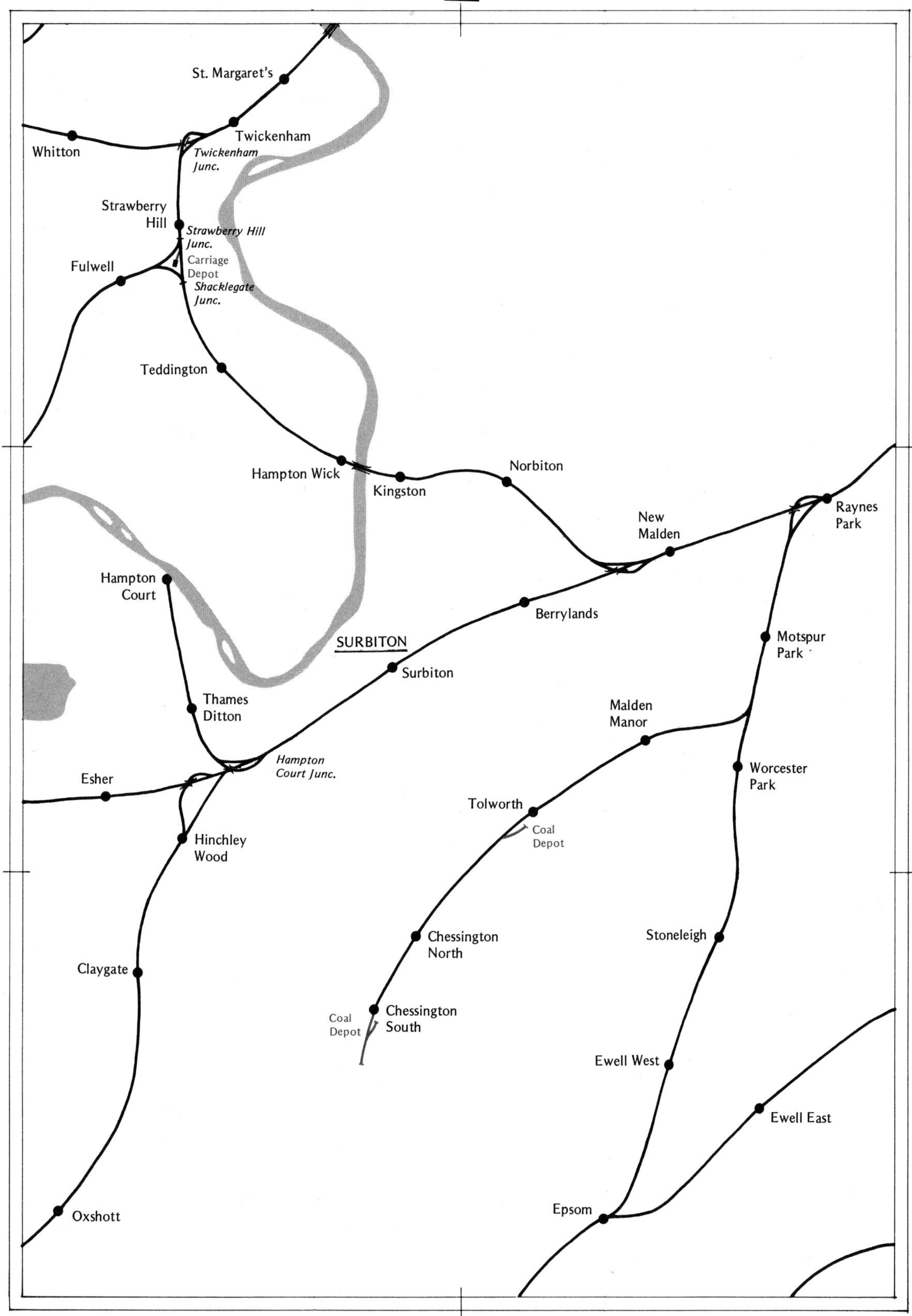

Twickenham

Whitton

Twickenham Junc.

Strawberry Hill

Strawberry Hill Junc.

Carriage Depot

Shacklegate Junc.

Fulwell

A

Teddington

Hampton Wick

Kingston

Norbiton

New Malden

Raynes Park

Hampton Court

Berrylands

Motspur Park

17

SURBITON

Surbiton

Malden Manor

Thames Ditton

Hampton Court Junc.

B

Esher

Tolworth

Coal Depot

Worcester Park

Hinchley Wood

Chessington North

Stoneleigh

Claygate

Coal Depot

Chessington South

Ewell West

Ewell East

C

Oxshott

Epsom

0 1 2 m.

0 1 2 3 km.

D

Southfields

Wandsworth
Common

Earlsfield

Balham

*Clapham
South*

N

*Balham
Junc.*

Streatham
Hill

Herne Hill N. Junc.

Herne
Hill

S. Junc.

North
Dulwich

Tulse
Hill

*Knight's
Hill
Tunnel*

West
Dulwich

*Leigham
Junc.*

*West Norwood
Junc.*

West
Norwood

Sydenham
Hill

D

WD

*Wimbledon
Park*

Wimbledon
Staff Halt

*Tooting
Bec*

E.M.U.
Depot

*Streatham
Hill Tun.*

Leigham Tun.

Streatham Tun.

*Penge Tunnel
(1 m. 381 yds)*

A

Haydons
Road

*Tooting
Broadway*

Tooting

*Streatham
Juncs.* *N.*

Streatham

S. Streatham
Common

Gipsy
Hill

Wimbledon

*South
Wimbledon*

*Collier's
Wood*

Merton
Abbey

Norbury

Crystal
Palace

Merton
Park

Wimbledon
Chase

N

Morden
Road

*Bromley
Junc.*

South
Merton

Morden

Thornton
Heath

Norwood
Junction

Morden
South

Milk
Depot

Depot

Mitcham

St. Helier

Mitcham
Junction

Beddington
Lane

Selhurst   SU

Selhurst Junc.
Gloucester Rd. Junc.
Gloryhole Junc.
St. James Junc.

*Norwood
Fork Junc.*

*Woodside
Junc.*

16

B

Sutton
Common

Hackbridge

Waddon
Marsh

*Windmill
Bridge Junc.*

West
Croydon

Depot

Addiscombe

East
Croydon

Bingham
Road

West
Sutton

Carshalton

Waddon

South
Croydon

Coombe
Road

Cheam

Sutton

Wallington

Selsdon

Carshalton
Beeches

Purley
Oaks

Sanderstead

Belmont

Purley

Coal Depot

Riddlesdown

C

Reedham

*Riddlesdown
Tunnel*

Banstead

Kenley

17

B BAKERLOO
C CENTRAL
O CIRCLE
D DISTRICT
F FLEET

1

M   METROPOLITAN
M(EL) METROPOLITAN (East London)
N   NORTHERN
P   PICCADILLY
V   VICTORIA

2

0   1   2 m.

0   1   2   3 km.

(1:70,000)

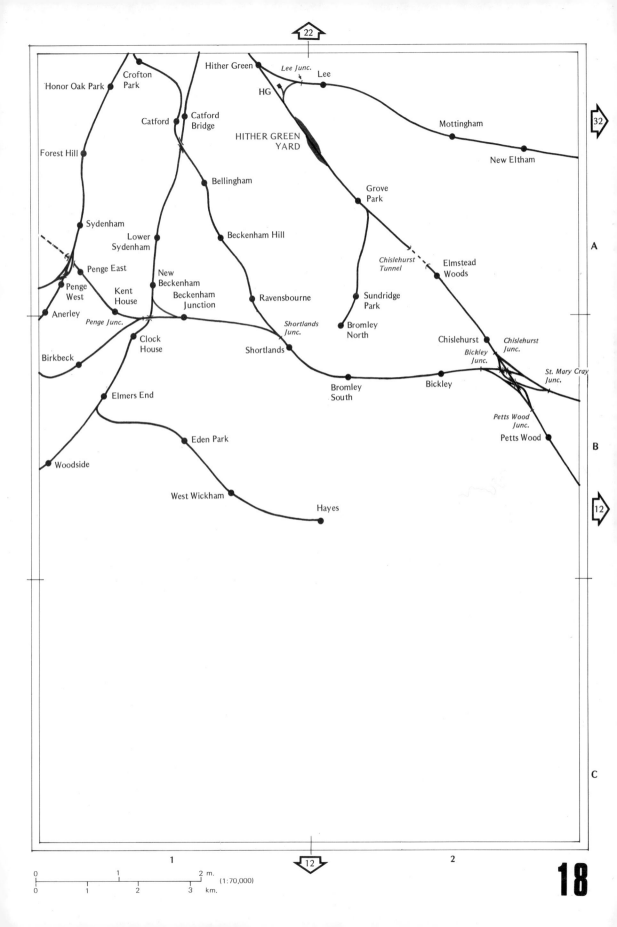

Honor Oak Park

Crofton Park

Hither Green

Lee Junc.

Lee

HG

Mottingham

Catford

Catford Bridge

HITHER GREEN YARD

New Eltham

Forest Hill

Bellingham

Grove Park

Sydenham

Beckenham Hill

Lower Sydenham

Chislehurst Tunnel

Elmstead Woods

A

Penge East

New Beckenham

Penge West

Kent House

Beckenham Junction

Ravensbourne

Sundridge Park

Anerley

Penge Junc.

Shortlands Junc.

Bromley North

Chislehurst

Chislehurst Junc.

Birkbeck

Clock House

Shortlands

Bickley Junc.

St. Mary Cray Junc.

Bromley South

Bickley

Elmers End

Petts Wood Junc.

Eden Park

Petts Wood

B

Woodside

West Wickham

Hayes

C

1

2

0   1   2 m.   (1:70,000)

0   1   2   3 km.

18

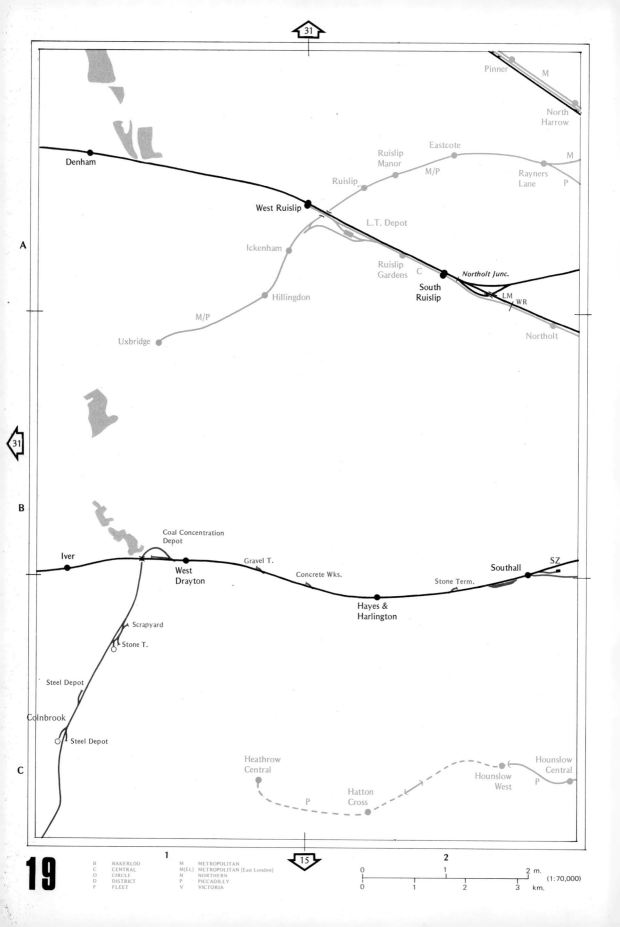

Pinner   M

North
Harrow

Denham

Eastcote

Ruislip
Manor

Ruislip   M/P

Rayners
Lane   M

P

West Ruislip

L.T. Depot

A

Ickenham

Ruislip
Gardens   C

South
Ruislip

Northolt Junc.

LM

WR

Hillingdon

M/P

Northolt

Uxbridge

31

B

Coal Concentration
Depot

Iver

West
Drayton

Gravel T.

Concrete Wks.

Stone Term.

Southall   SZ

Hayes &
Harlington

Scrapyard

Stone T.

Steel Depot

Colnbrook

Steel Depot

C

Heathrow
Central

Hatton
Cross   P

Hounslow
West   P

Hounslow
Central

19

B	BAKERLOO	M	METROPOLITAN
C	CENTRAL	M(EL)	METROPOLITAN (East London)
O	CIRCLE	N	NORTHERN
D	DISTRICT	P	PICCADILLY
F	FLEET	V	VICTORIA

0   1   2 m.

0   1   2   3   km.

(1:70,000)

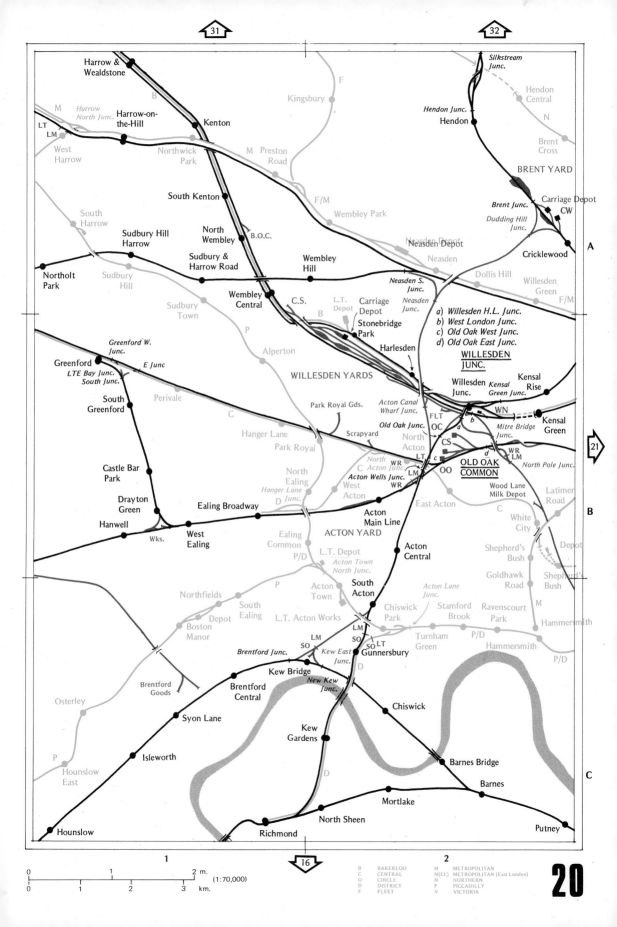

21

Silkstream Junc.

Hendon Junc.
Hendon

BRENT YARD

Harrow &
Wealdstone

Kenton

Harrow
North Junc.
M

LT
LM

West
Harrow

Harrow-on-
the-Hill

Northwick
Park

Kingsbury

F

Hendon
Central

N

Brent
Cross

Carriage Depot
CW

Brent Junc.

Dudding Hill
Junc.

Cricklewood

A

South Kenton

North
Wembley

B.O.C.

Preston
Road

Wembley Park

F/M

Neasden Depot

Neasden

Dollis Hill

Willesden
Green

F/M

Sudbury Hill
Harrow

Sudbury &
Harrow Road

Wembley
Hill

C.S.

Neasden S.
Junc.

Neasden
Junc.

South
Harrow

Sudbury
Hill

Wembley
Central

L.T.
Depot

Carriage
Depot

a) Willesden H.L. Junc.
b) West London Junc.
c) Old Oak West Junc.
d) Old Oak East Junc.

WILLESDEN
JUNC.

Northolt
Park

M

Sudbury
Town

Alperton

P

B

Stonebridge
Park

Harlesden

WILLESDEN YARDS

Willesden
Junc.

Kensal
Green Junc.

Kensal
Rise

Greenford W.
Junc.

LTE Bay Junc.
South Junc.

E Junc.

Perivale

C

Park Royal Gds.

Acton Canal
Wharf Junc.

Old Oak Junc.

FLT

OC

a

b

WN

Mitre Bridge
Junc.

Kensal
Green

Greenford

South
Greenford

Hanger Lane

Park Royal

Scrapyard

North
Acton

CS

d

c

WR
LM

North Pole Junc.

Castle Bar
Park

North
Hanger Lane
Junc.

North
C. Acton Junc.

WR

Acton Wells Junc.
WR

LT

LM

OO

Wood Lane
Milk Depot

Latimer
Road

B

Drayton
Green

Hanwell

West
Ealing

Ealing Broadway

Wks.

North
Ealing

West
Acton

East Acton

C

White
City

Depot

Shepherd's
Bush

Shepherd's
Bush

Ealing
Common

P/D

Acton
Main Line

ACTON YARD

Acton
Central

Goldhawk
Road

Northfields

L.T. Depot

Acton Town
North Junc.

P

Acton
Town

South
Acton

South
Ealing

L.T. Acton Works

Chiswick
Park

Acton Lane
Junc.

Stamford
Brook

Ravenscourt
Park

M

Hammersmith

Osterley

Boston
Manor

P

LM

SO

Brentford Junc.

Kew East
Junc.

LM
SO

SO LT

Gunnersbury

Turnham
Green

D

Hammersmith

P/D

P/D

Kew Bridge

New Kew
Junc.

Brentford
Goods

Brentford
Central

Chiswick

Syon Lane

Kew
Gardens

Barnes Bridge

C

Isleworth

D

Barnes

Hounslow
East

P

Mortlake

Putney

Hounslow

Richmond

North Sheen

0   1   2 m.
0   1   2   3 km.   (1:70,000)

1

2

B   BAKERLOO   M   METROPOLITAN
C   CENTRAL   M(EL) METROPOLITAN (East London)
C   CIRCLE   N   NORTHERN
D   DISTRICT   P   PICCADILLY
F   FLEET   V   VICTORIA

20

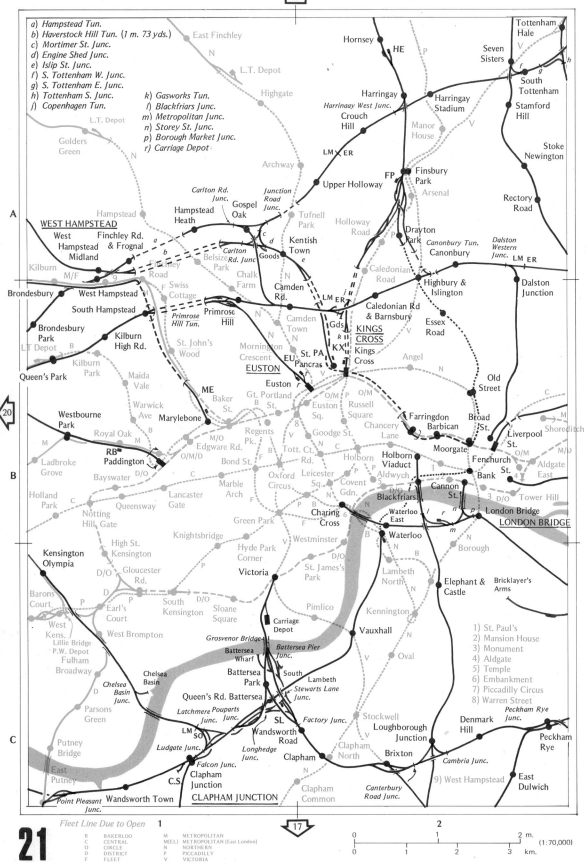

a) Hampstead Tun.
b) Haverstock Hill Tun. (1 m. 73 yds.)
c) Mortimer St. Junc.
d) Engine Shed Junc.
e) Islip St. Junc.
f) S. Tottenham W. Junc.
g) S. Tottenham E. Junc.
h) Tottenham S. Junc.
j) Copenhagen Tun.

k) Gasworks Tun.
l) Blackfriars Junc.
m) Metropolitan Junc.
n) Storey St. Junc.
p) Borough Market Junc.
r) Carriage Depot

East Finchley

Hornsey   HE

Tottenham Hale

Seven Sisters

South Tottenham

L.T. Depot

Highgate

Harringay

Harringay Stadium

Stamford Hill

Stoke Newington

Golders Green

L.T. Depot

Archway

Harringay West Junc.

Crouch Hill

Manor House

Rectory Road

Hampstead

LM × ER

Upper Holloway

Finsbury Park   FP

Arsenal

WEST HAMPSTEAD

Hampstead Heath

Gospel Oak

Tufnell Park

Holloway Road

Drayton Park

West Hampstead Midland

Finchley Rd. & Frognal

Carlton Rd. Junc.

Junction Road Junc.

Kentish Town

Canonbury Tun.

Dalston Western Junc.

Kilburn

M/F   9

Belsize Park

Carlton Rd. Junc.

Goods

Caledonian Road

Canonbury

LM ER

Brondesbury

West Hampstead

Finchley Road

Chalk Farm

Camden Rd.

Highbury & Islington

Dalston Junction

South Hampstead

Swiss Cottage

LM ER

Caledonian Rd & Barnsbury

Brondesbury Park

Primrose Hill Tun.

Primrose Hill

Camden Town

Gds

KINGS CROSS

Essex Road

Kilburn High Rd.

St. John's Wood

KX

Kilburn Park

Mornington Crescent

St. PA

Kings Cross

Angel

Old Street

Queen's Park

EU

EUSTON

Pancras

LT Depot

Maida Vale

Euston

r

Broad St.

Shoreditch

Westbourne Park

Warwick Ave

Marylebone   ME

Baker St.

Gt. Portland St.

Euston Sq.

Russell Square

Farringdon

Barbican

Liverpool St.

Royal Oak

Edgware Rd.

Regents Pk.

Chancery Lane

Moorgate

Fenchurch St.

Ladbroke Grove

RB

Paddington

M/O

Goodge St.

Holborn

Aldgate East

Bayswater

D/O

Bond St.

Tott. Ct. Rd.

Holborn Viaduct

Bank

Holland Park

Queensway

Lancaster Gate

Marble Arch

Oxford Circus

Leicester Sq.

Covent Gdn.

Aldwych

Cannon St.

Tower Hill

Notting Hill Gate

Blackfriars

Charing Cross

Waterloo East

London Bridge

LONDON BRIDGE

Kensington Olympia

High St. Kensington

Green Park

Westminster

Waterloo

Borough

Barons Court

Gloucester Rd.

Hyde Park Corner

St. James's Park

Lambeth North

Elephant & Castle

Bricklayer's Arms

West Kens.

Earl's Court

South Kensington

Victoria

Pimlico

Kennington

Lillie Bridge P.W. Depot

Sloane Square

Fulham Broadway

Carriage Depot

Vauxhall

Oval

1) St. Paul's
2) Mansion House
3) Monument
4) Aldgate
5) Temple
6) Embankment
7) Piccadilly Circus
8) Warren Street

Chelsea Basin

Grosvenor Bridge

Battersea Wharf

Battersea Pier Junc.

Chelsea Basin Junc.

Battersea Park

South Lambeth

Stockwell

Denmark Hill

Peckham Rye Junc.

Parsons Green

Queen's Rd. Battersea

Stewarts Lane Junc.

Loughborough Junction

Peckham Rye

Putney Bridge

Latchmere Junc.

Pouparts Junc.

SL

Factory Junc.

Clapham North

Brixton

Cambria Junc.

East Putney

LM   SO

Wandsworth Road

Longhedge Junc.

Clapham

9) West Hampstead

East Dulwich

Ludgate Junc.

Falcon Junc.

C.S.

Clapham Junction

CLAPHAM JUNCTION

Clapham Common

Canterbury Road Junc.

Point Pleasant Junc.

Wandsworth Town

Fleet Line Due to Open   1

B   BAKERLOO
C   CENTRAL
O   CIRCLE
D   DISTRICT
F   FLEET

M   METROPOLITAN
M(EL) METROPOLITAN (East London)
N   NORTHERN
P   PICCADILLY
V   VICTORIA

0   1   2 m.

0   1   2   3   km.

(1:70,000)

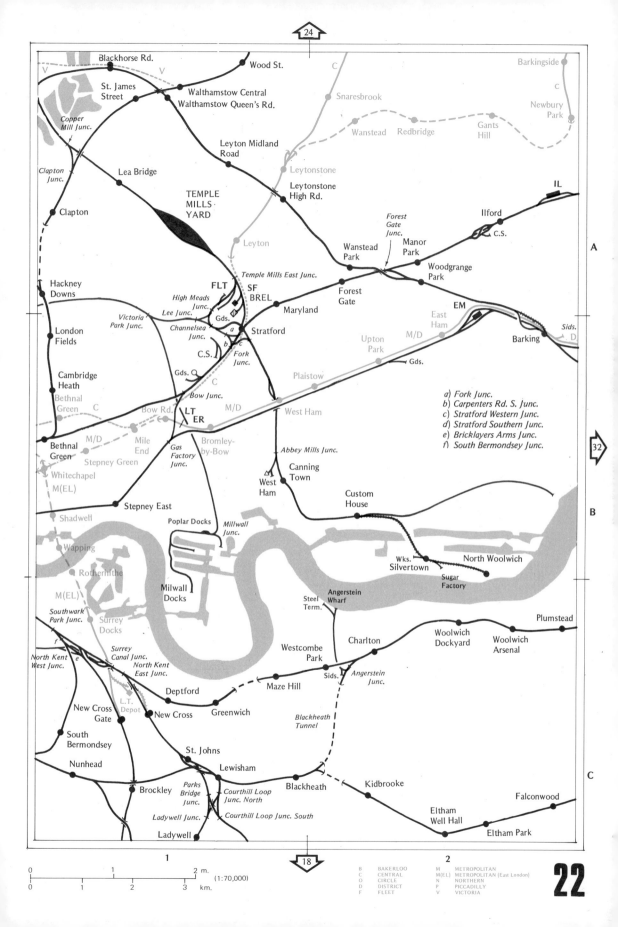

Blackhorse Rd.
Wood St.
Barkingside
St. James Street
Walthamstow Central
Walthamstow Queen's Rd.
Snaresbrook
C
Newbury Park
Copper Mill Junc.
Leyton Midland Road
Wanstead
Redbridge
Gants Hill
Clapton Junc.
Lea Bridge
Leytonstone
Leytonstone High Rd.
IL
Clapton
TEMPLE MILLS YARD
Leyton
Ilford
C.S.
Forest Gate Junc.
Wanstead Park
Manor Park
Woodgrange Park
A
Hackney Downs
Temple Mills East Junc.
FLT
SF BREL
Maryland
Forest Gate
EM
High Meads Junc.
Lee Junc.
East Ham
Victoria Park Junc.
Gds.
a
Stratford
M/D
Barking
Sids.
London Fields
Channelsea Junc.
b c
Upton Park
D
Cambridge Heath
C.S.
Fork Junc.
Gds.
Bethnal Green
Gds.
Plaistow
C
a) Fork Junc.
b) Carpenters Rd. S. Junc.
c) Stratford Western Junc.
d) Stratford Southern Junc.
e) Bricklayers Arms Junc.
f) South Bermondsey Junc.
Bow Junc.
M/D
West Ham
Bethnal Green
M/D
Mile End
Bow Rd.
LT ER
Bromley-by-Bow
Whitechapel
M(EL)
Stepney Green
Gas Factory Junc.
Abbey Mills Junc.
Canning Town
Shadwell
Stepney East
Poplar Docks
Millwall Junc.
West Ham
Custom House
B
Wapping
Rotherhithe
Silvertown
Wks.
North Woolwich
M(EL)
Milwall Docks
Sugar Factory
Southwark Park Junc.
Surrey Docks
Angerstein Wharf
Steel Term.
Plumstead
f
North Kent West Junc.
e
Surrey Canal Junc.
North Kent East Junc.
Westcombe Park
Charlton
Woolwich Dockyard
Woolwich Arsenal
L.T. Depot
Deptford
New Cross
Greenwich
Maze Hill
Sids.
Angerstein Junc.
New Cross Gate
South Bermondsey
St. Johns
Blackheath Tunnel
Kidbrooke
Falconwood
C
Nunhead
Lewisham
Blackheath
Brockley
Parks Bridge Junc.
Courthill Loop Junc. North
Eltham Well Hall
Eltham Park
Ladywell Junc.
Courthill Loop Junc. South
Ladywell

1 2

0   1   2 m.
0 1 2 3 km.
(1:70,000)

B	BAKERLOO	M	METROPOLITAN
C	CENTRAL	M(EL)	METROPOLITAN (East London)
O	CIRCLE	N	NORTHERN
D	DISTRICT	P	PICCADILLY
F	FLEET	V	VICTORIA

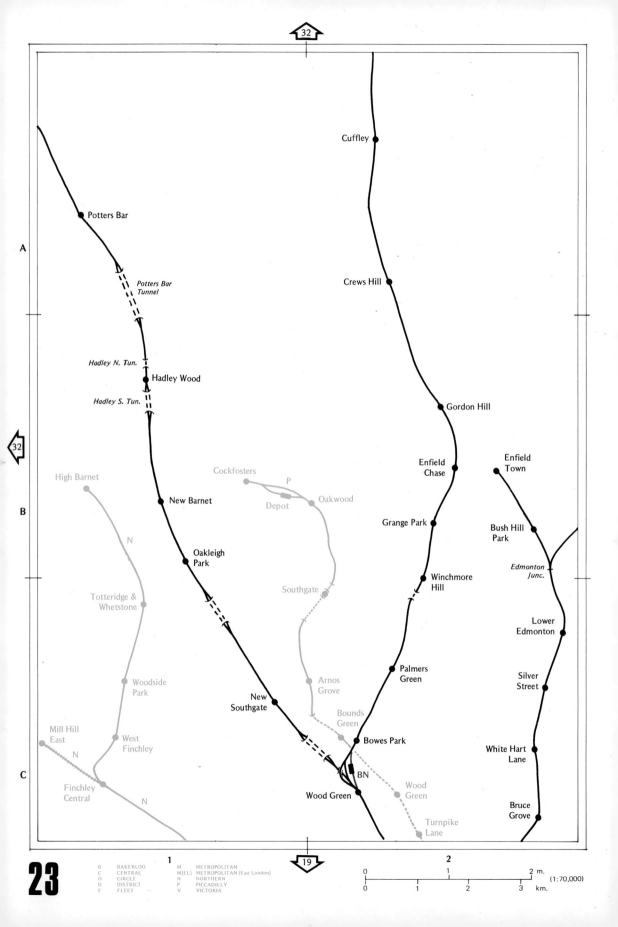

Cuffley

Potters Bar

A

Potters Bar
Tunnel

Crews Hill

Hadley N. Tun.

Hadley Wood

Gordon Hill

Hadley S. Tun.

Enfield
Chase

Enfield
Town

High Barnet

Cockfosters

P

B

New Barnet

Depot

Oakwood

Grange Park

Bush Hill
Park

N

Edmonton
Junc.

Oakleigh
Park

Totteridge &
Whetstone

Southgate

Winchmore
Hill

Lower
Edmonton

Woodside
Park

Arnos
Grove

Palmers
Green

Silver
Street

New
Southgate

Bounds
Green

Mill Hill
East

West
Finchley

Bowes Park

White Hart
Lane

C

N

BN

Wood
Green

Finchley
Central

N

Wood Green

Bruce
Grove

Turnpike
Lane

23

B	BAKERLOO	M	METROPOLITAN
C	CENTRAL	M(EL)	METROPOLITAN (East London)
O	CIRCLE	N	NORTHERN
D	DISTRICT	P	PICCADILLY
F	FLEET	V	VICTORIA

1

2

0   1   2 m.

(1:70,000)

0   1   2   3   km.

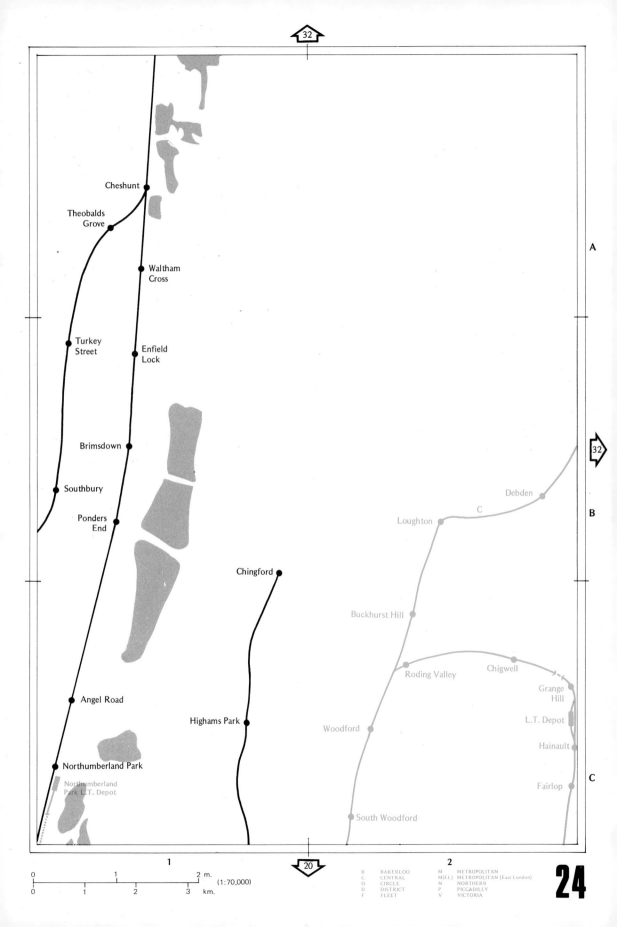

32

Cheshunt

Theobalds
Grove

Waltham
Cross

A

Turkey
Street

Enfield
Lock

Brimsdown

32

Southbury

Debden

C

B

Loughton

Ponders
End

Chingford

Buckhurst Hill

Chigwell

Roding Valley

Grange
Hill

L.T. Depot

Angel Road

Hainault

Highams Park

Woodford

Northumberland Park

Fairlop

Northumberland
Park L.T. Depot

C

South Woodford

1

2

20

B	BAKERLOO	M	METROPOLITAN
C	CENTRAL	M(EL)	METROPOLITAN (East London)
O	CIRCLE	N	NORTHERN
D	DISTRICT	P	PICCADILLY
F	FLEET	V	VICTORIA

24

0   1   2 m.

0   1   2   3 km.   (1:70,000)

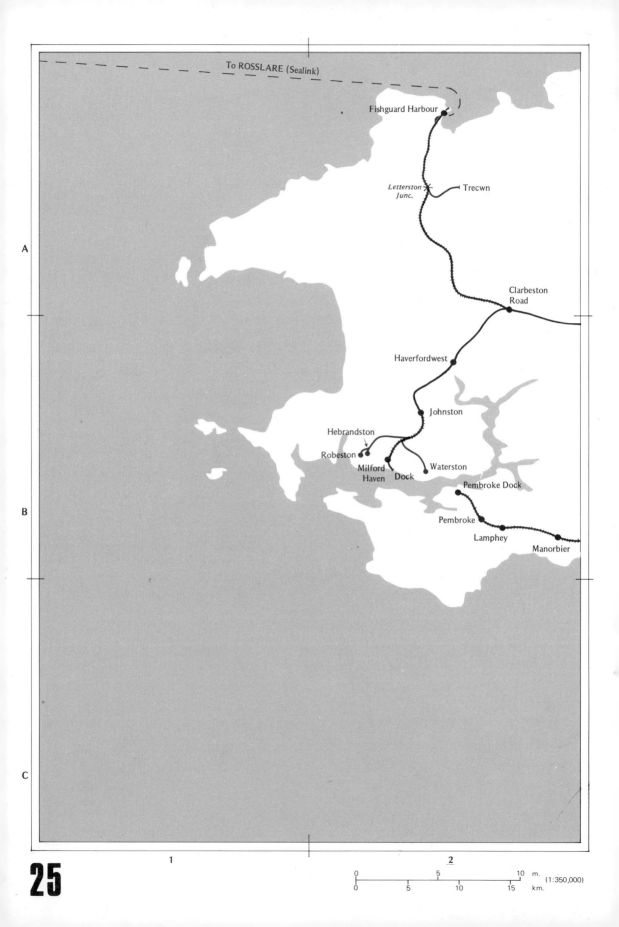

To ROSSLARE (Sealink)

Fishguard Harbour

Letterston Junc. Trecwn

Clarbeston Road

Haverfordwest

Johnston

Hebrandston

Robeston

Milford Haven

Dock Waterston

Pembroke Dock

Pembroke

Lamphey

Manorbier

25

1

2

0   5   10 m.

0   5   10   15 km.

(1:350,000)

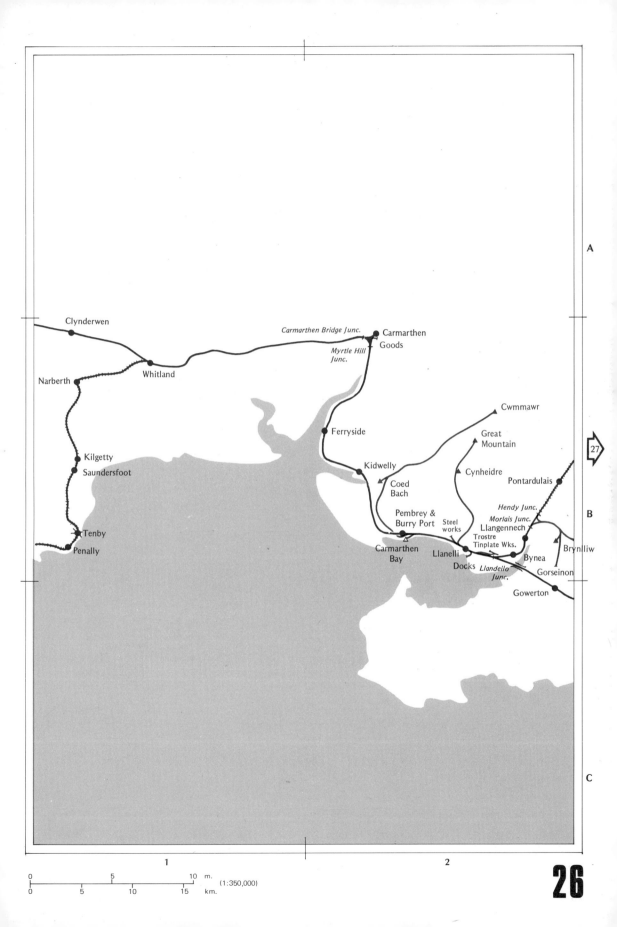

Clynderwen

Carmarthen Bridge Junc.   Carmarthen
Goods

Myrtle Hill
Junc.

Narberth   Whitland

Cwmmawr

Ferryside

Great
Mountain

Kilgetty

Saundersfoot

Kidwelly

Cynheidre

Pontardulais

Coed
Bach

Hendy Junc.

Pembrey &
Burry Port

Morlais Junc.

Steel
works

Llangennech

Trostre
Tinplate Wks.

Tenby

B

Penally

Carmarthen
Bay

Llanelli

Brynlliw

Docks

Bynea

Llandeila
Junc.

Gorseinon

Gowerton

27

A

C

1   2

0   5   10 m.
0   5   10   15 km.   (1:350,000)

26

35

Llanwrtyd Wells Llangammarch Wells

Sugar Loaf Tun. (Summit)

Cynghordy

Llandovery

Llanwrda

Llangadog

A

Llandeilo
Ffairfach

Llandybie

Ammanford

26

Pantyffynon

Gwauncaegurwen

Craig-y-nos

Abernant

Onllwyn

Aberpergwm

Penderyn

Resolven

Tower

1) Pontlottyn
2) Merthyr Vale
3) Quaker's Yard
4) Merthyr Vale
5) Trehafod
6) Wagon Works
7) Car Works
8) Jersey Marine
a) Jersey Marine North Junc.
b) Dynevor Junc.
c) Jersey Marine South Junc.

Dowlais Rhymmney

Merthyr

1

Cwm Bargoed

Graig Merthyr

B

Velindre Tinplate Works

Monds Nickel Works

Blaenant

Neath & Brecon Junc.

Morriston

Landore Junc.

LE

Swansea Loop Juncs.

Llandarcy

Swansea

Jersey Marine

E. Dock

8 7 FLT

6

Baglan Bay

Neath
Wks.

Court Sart Junc.
Briton Ferry
Steelworks
Chem. Wks.

Caerau

Nant-y-Moel

Maesteg

Llynfi

Aberdare
Aberdare*

Pentrebach

Troedyrhiw

Mountain Ash

Phurnacite Plant

Penrhiwceider

4

2

New town

Taff Merthyr

Black Lion
Treharris

Nelson

Treherbert

Maerdy

Cwmparc

Treorchy

Ystrad Rhondda

Lady Windsor

Llwynypia

Tonypandy

Dinas Rhonnda

Porth

Trehafod

Abercynon

Abercynon

3

5

Windsor

Pontypridd
Treforest

Nantgarw

PORT TALBOT

Port Talbot

Docks

Steelworks

MARGAM YARD

MG

To CORK
(B. & I.)

Margam Middle Junc.
Margam Moors Junc.
Mill Pit

Tondu

Ogmore Junc.

Newlands Junc.

Water St. Junc.

Bridgend

Coed Ely

Mwyndy Junc.

Llanharan
Llantrisant

Cwm

Common Junc.

Creigiau

Treforest Estate

C

1

7

2

0   5   10 m.

0   5   10   15 km.

(1:350,000)

27

Shelwick Junc.

Bulmer's Wks. HF
Hereford

1) Bargoed
2) Gilfach Fargoed
3) Radyr
4) Coryton
5) Whitchurch (South Glam)
6) Rhiwbina
7) Birchgrove
8) Heath Low Level
9) Heath High Level
10) Llandaff for Whitchurch
11) Grangetown (South Glam)
12) Ninian Park
13) Bargoed Coll.
14) Britannia Coll.
15) Penallta Coll.
16) Ferry Road

a) *Walnut Tree Junc.*
b) *Leckwith Juncs.*
c) *Gaer Junc.*
d) *Alexandra Dock Juncs.*
e) *Ebbw Junc.*

f) *Hallen Marsh Junc.*

A

Abergavenny

29

Parkend

Ebbw Vale
(Steelworks)

Blaenavon

B

Rose
Heyworth

Lydney

Marine

Tir Phil
Markham   Six Bells
Brithdir   Aberbeeg

Glascoed
Little Mill Junc.

1 ▲ 13
2   *Panteg &
*   *C Junc.*
Pengam ○ ▲ 14   Oakdale
15   Celynen North

Hafodyrynys

Pontypool
East Junc.
Steelworks

Tintern □
Tidenham Tun.
Tidenham □

Hengoed
Ystrad
Mynach   Celynen South
Llanbradach
Bedwas   *Lime Kiln Junc.*

Llantarnam Junc.

Chepstow ● Wks.

Caerwent

Wks. Machen   NEWPORT
Aber   Caerphilly △ Rogerstone   Newport
Wks.   *Bassaleg Junc.* *Maindee Juncs.*
Caerphilly Tun.   c   *East Usk Junc. & Yard*
(1 m. 173 yds.)   *Park Junc.* E   Wks.
Cefn On   d
Taffs   Llanishen   Dks.   Wks.
Well   Llanwern
a 4 5 6 7 8 *Long*   Aluminium Works Steelworks
3   9 *Dyke*
10   Coal *Junc.*
Dep   Wks.
Queen St.   b   Pengam FLT
Cardiff Cen.
Wks.   Steelworks
12 11 CF Bute Rd.
16   Docks

Severn Tunnel
Junction
            Sudbrook
ST Caldicot *Severn Tunnel (4m 628yds.)*

Severn   Pilning
Beach   *Patchway
*   *Tunnels*

St. Andrew's
Road   Chem. Wks.
Docks   Patchway   Bristol
f   Parkway
Avonmouth Wks. N. Filton Plat.*
Docks   Coal Filton
Shirehampton Depot
Portishead △   Sea Mills

Clifton Down   Stapleton
Road

C

1   8   2   *SEE INSET PAGE 8*

0 ———— 5 ———— 10 m.
0 — 5 — 10 — 15 km.
(1:350,000)

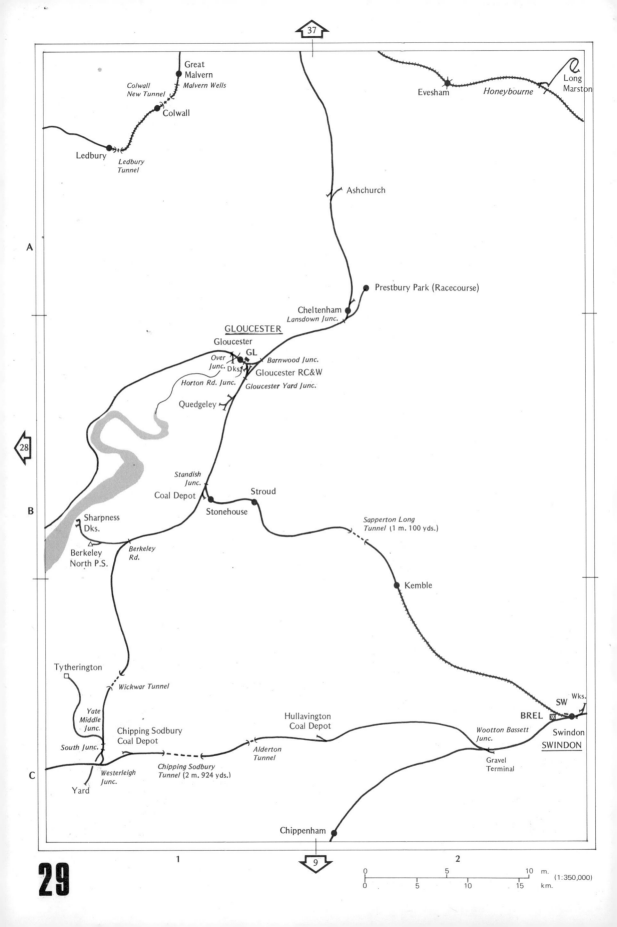

37

Great
Malvern
Colwall *Malvern Wells*
New Tunnel
Colwall

Ledbury
Ledbury
Tunnel

Evesham *Honeybourne* Long
Marston

Ashchurch

A

Prestbury Park (Racecourse)

Cheltenham
Lansdown Junc.

GLOUCESTER
Gloucester
GL
Over Barnwood Junc.
Junc. Dks.
Gloucester RC&W
Horton Rd. Junc. *Gloucester Yard Junc.*

Quedgeley

28

Standish
Junc. Stroud
Coal Depot
Stonehouse *Sapperton Long*
Tunnel (1 m. 100 yds.)

B

Sharpness
Dks.
Berkeley
Rd.
Berkeley
North P.S.

Kemble

Tytherington
Wickwar Tunnel

Yate
Middle
Junc.
Hullavington
Coal Depot
Chipping Sodbury
Coal Depot
Wootton Bassett
Junc.
SW Wks.
South Junc.
BREL
Swindon
Alderton SWINDON
Tunnel
Gravel
Terminal
Westerleigh *Chipping Sodbury*
C *Junc.* *Tunnel (2 m. 924 yds.)*
Yard

Chippenham

29

1   9   2

0   5   10 m.
                                              (1:350,000)
0   5   10   15 km.

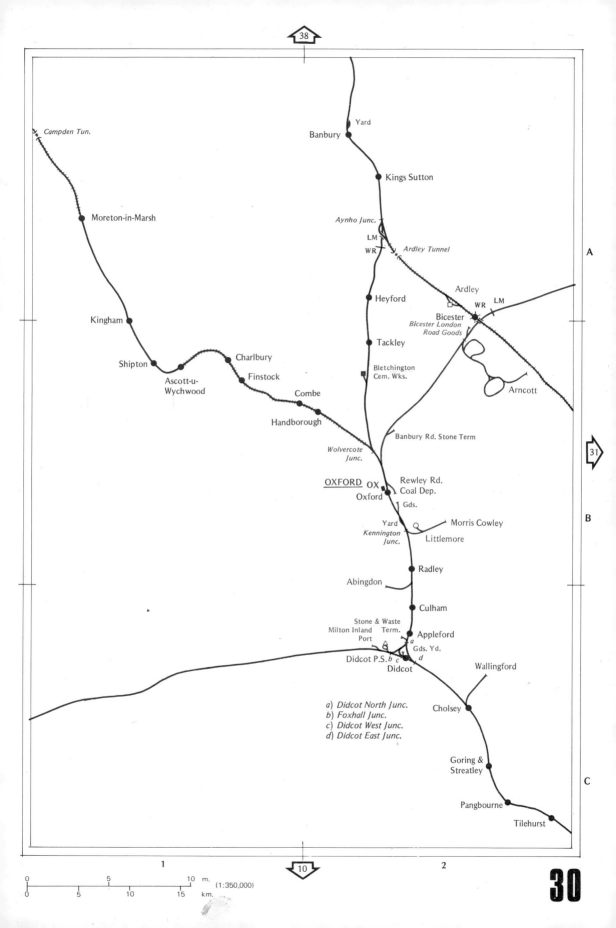

Campden Tun.

Banbury
Yard

Kings Sutton

Moreton-in-Marsh

Aynho Junc.
LM
WR
Ardley Tunnel

Ardley
Bicester
WR LM
Bicester London
Road Goods

Heyford

Kingham

Tackley

Charlbury
Shipton
Finstock
Ascott-u-
Wychwood

Bletchington
Cem. Wks.

Arncott

Combe

Handborough

Banbury Rd. Stone Term

Wolvercote
Junc.

OXFORD OX
Oxford

Rewley Rd.
Coal Dep.

Gds.

Yard
Kennington
Junc.

Morris Cowley

Littlemore

Abingdon

Radley

Culham

Stone & Waste
Milton Inland   Term.
Port

Appleford
a
Gds. Yd.
b c
d

Didcot P.S.

Wallingford

Didcot

a) Didcot North Junc.
b) Foxhall Junc.
c) Didcot West Junc.
d) Didcot East Junc.

Cholsey

Goring &
Streatley

Pangbourne

Tilehurst

1

2

0   5   10   m.   (1:350,000)
0   5   10   15   km.

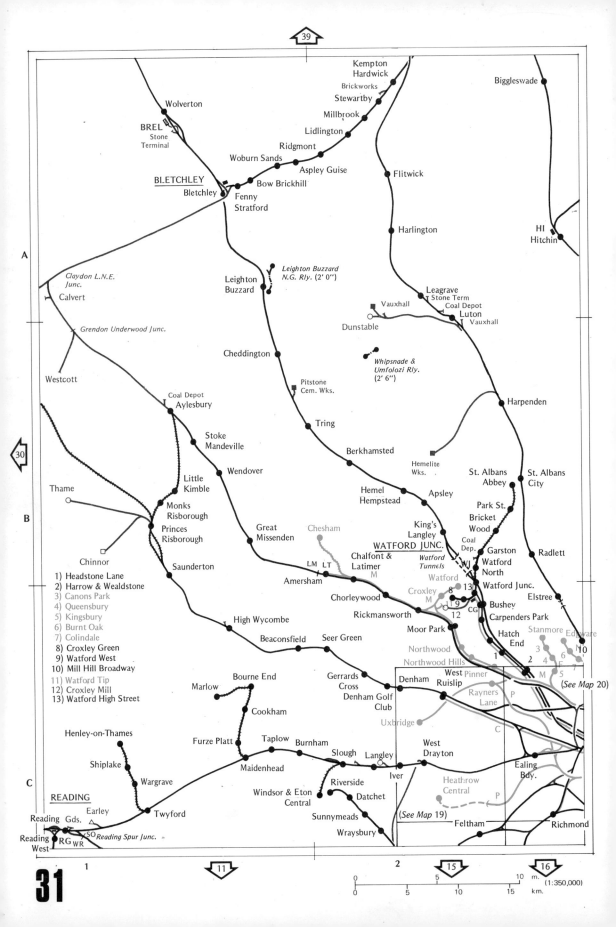

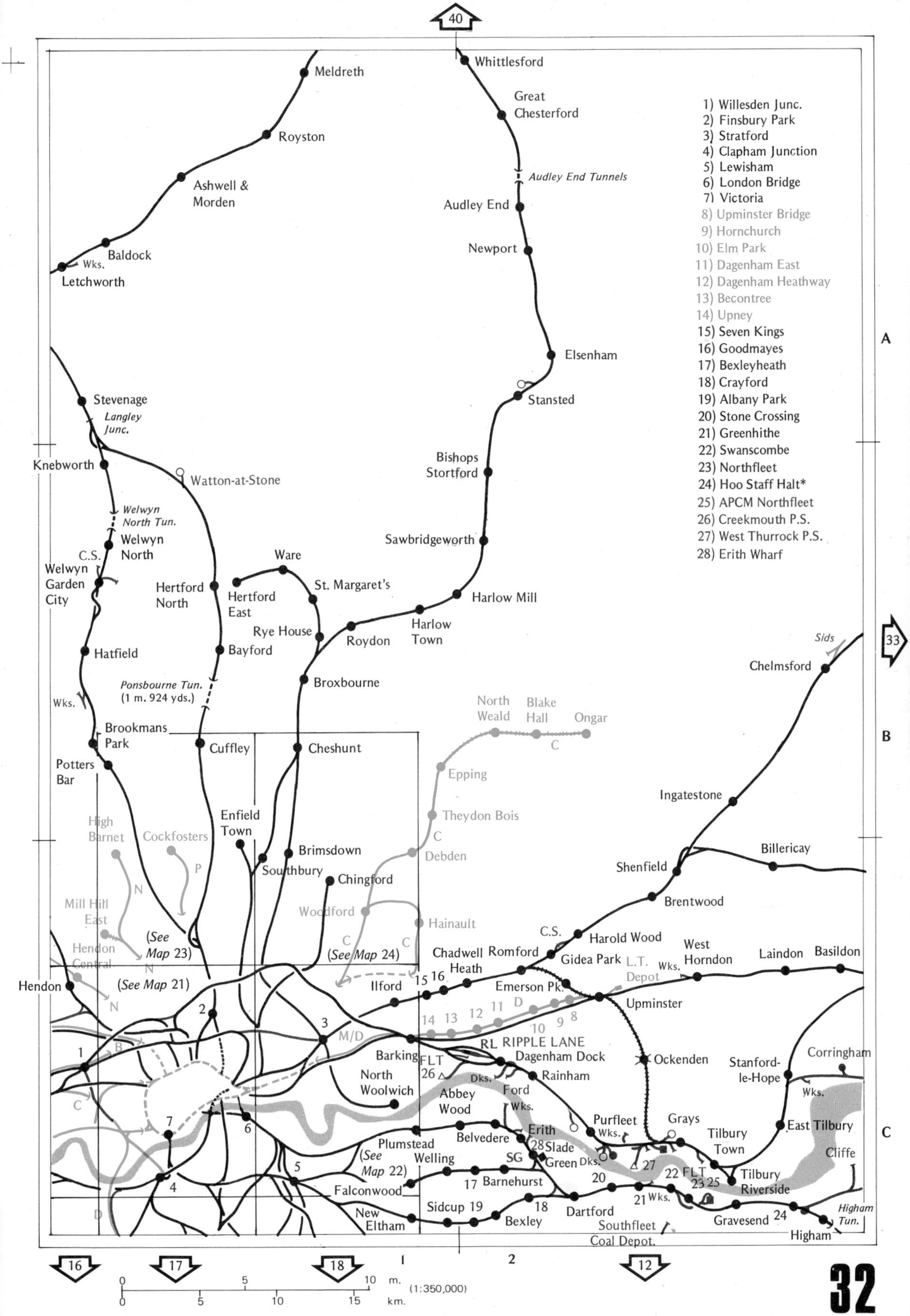
40
Whittlesford
Meldreth
Great Chesterford
Royston
Ashwell & Morden
Audley End Tunnels
Audley End
Newport
Baldock
Wks.
Letchworth
1) Willesden Junc.
2) Finsbury Park
3) Stratford
4) Clapham Junction
5) Lewisham
6) London Bridge
7) Victoria
8) Upminster Bridge
9) Hornchurch
10) Elm Park
11) Dagenham East
12) Dagenham Heathway
13) Becontree
14) Upney
15) Seven Kings
16) Goodmayes
17) Bexleyheath
18) Crayford
19) Albany Park
20) Stone Crossing
21) Greenhithe
22) Swanscombe
23) Northfleet
24) Hoo Staff Halt*
25) APCM Northfleet
26) Creekmouth P.S.
27) West Thurrock P.S.
28) Erith Wharf
A
Elsenham
Stansted
Stevenage
Langley Junc.
Knebworth
Watton-at-Stone
Bishops Stortford
Welwyn North Tun.
Welwyn North
C.S.
Welwyn Garden City
Sawbridgeworth
Ware
Hertford North
Hertford East
St. Margaret's
Harlow Mill
Rye House
Roydon
Harlow Town
Hatfield
Bayford
Sids
33
Chelmsford
Broxbourne
Ponsbourne Tun. (1 m. 924 yds.)
Wks.
North Weald
Blake Hall
Ongar
C
Brookmans Park
Cuffley
Cheshunt
B
Potters Bar
Epping
Ingatestone
High Barnet
Enfield Town
Theydon Bois
Cockfosters
C
Debden
Billericay
Brimsdown
P
Southbury
Shenfield
Chingford
N
Mill Hill East
Woodford
Brentwood
Hainault
(See Map 23)
C.S.
Harold Wood
Hendon Central
C
C
(See Map 24)
Chadwell Heath
Romford
Gidea Park
L.T. Depot
Wks.
West Horndon
Laindon
Basildon
Hendon
(See Map 21)
N
Ilford
15
16
Emerson Pk.
D
Upminster
N
2
14
13
12
11
10
9
8
3
M/D
RL
RIPPLE LANE
1
B
Barking
FLT
Dagenham Dock
Ockenden
Stanford-le-Hope
Corringham
26
North Woolwich
Dks.
Rainham
Wks.
C
Abbey Wood
Ford
Wks.
7
6
Erith
Purfleet
Wks.
Grays
Tilbury Town
East Tilbury
C
Plumstead
Belvedere
28
Slade Green
Dks.
(See Map 22)
Welling
SG
27
22
FLT
23
25
Tilbury Riverside
Cliffe
4
5
Falconwood
17
Barnehurst
20
21
Wks.
D
New Eltham
Sidcup
19
18
Dartford
Bexley
Southfleet Coal Depot
Gravesend
24
Higham Tun.
Higham
16
17
18
1
2
12
0
5
10
m.
(1:350,000)
0
5
10
15
km.

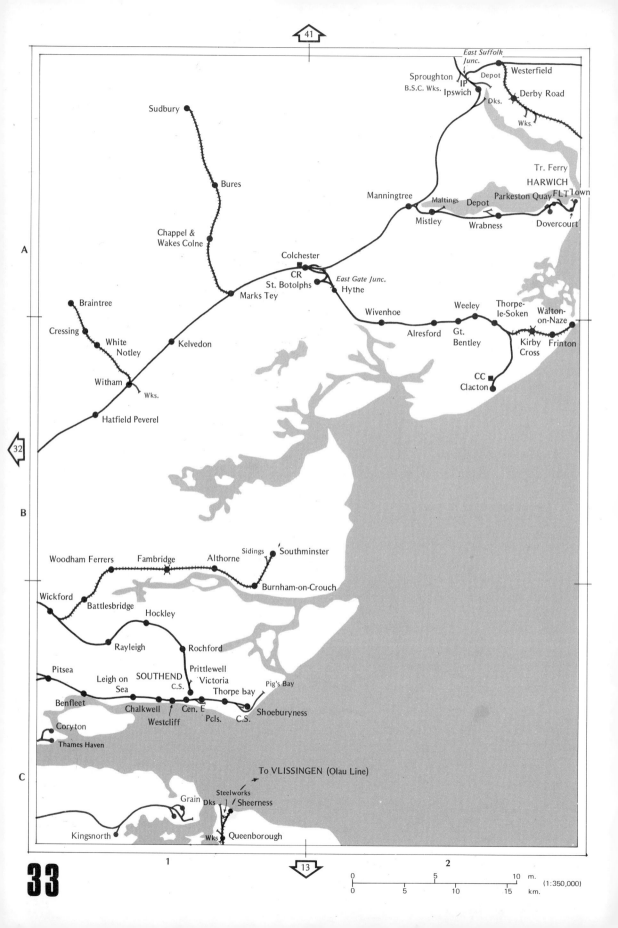

East Suffolk
Junc.

Westerfield

Sproughton
B.S.C. Wks.   Ipswich   IP   Depot
Dks.   Derby Road

Wks.

Tr. Ferry
HARWICH
Parkeston Quay   FLT Town
Dovercourt

Sudbury

Bures

Manningtree   Maltings   Depot
Mistley   Wrabness

Chappel &
Wakes Colne

Colchester
CR
St. Botolphs   East Gate Junc.
Marks Tey   Hythe

Weeley   Thorpe-
le-Soken   Walton-
on-Naze

Wivenhoe

Braintree
Cressing

Alresford   Gt.
Bentley   Kirby
Cross   Frinton

White
Notley   Kelvedon

CC
Clacton

Witham   Wks.

Hatfield Peverel

A

B

Sidings   Southminster
Woodham Ferrers   Fambridge   Althorne

Wickford   Burnham-on-Crouch
Battlesbridge

Hockley

Rayleigh   Rochford

Pitsea   Prittlewell
Leigh on   SOUTHEND   Victoria
Sea   C.S.   Pig's Bay
Thorpe bay

Benfleet   Chalkwell   Cen. E   Shoeburyness
Coryton   Westcliff   Pcls.   C.S.
Thames Haven

To VLISSINGEN (Olau Line)

C

Steelworks
Grain   Dks.   Sheerness

Kingsnorth   Wks.   Queenborough

1   2

33

0   5   10   m.
0   5   10   15   km.
(1:350,000)

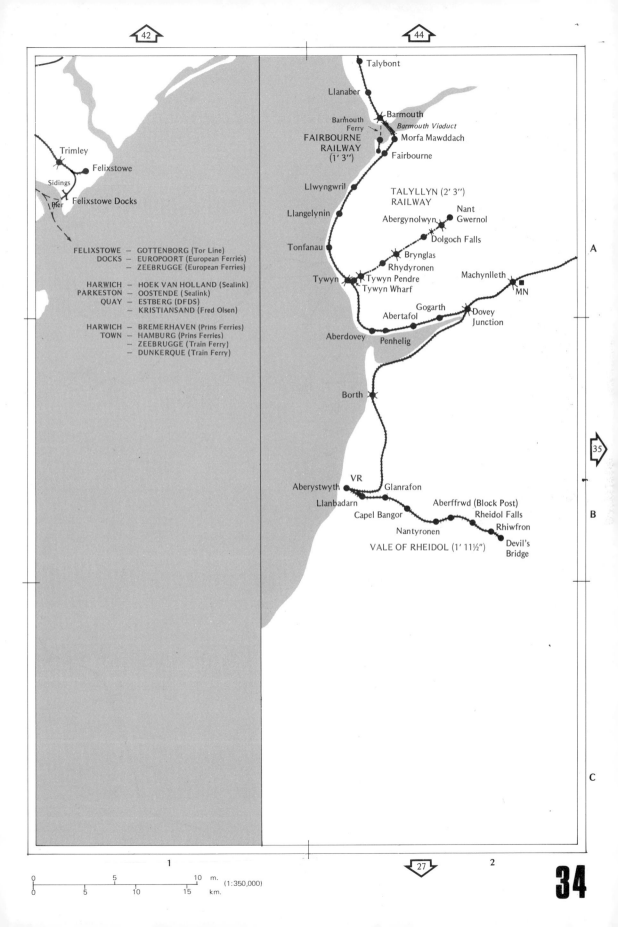

Talybont

Llanaber

Barmouth
Barmouth
Ferry
Barmouth Viaduct
FAIRBOURNE
RAILWAY
(1' 3")
Morfa Mawddach

Fairbourne

Trimley

Felixstowe

Sidings

Pier

Felixstowe Docks

Llwyngwril

Llangelynin

TALYLLYN (2' 3")
RAILWAY

Nant
Gwernol

Abergynolwyn

Dolgoch Falls

Tonfanau

Brynglas

Rhydyronen

A

Machynlleth

Tywyn

Tywyn Pendre
Tywyn Wharf

MN

FELIXSTOWE — GOTTENBORG (Tor Line)
DOCKS — EUROPOORT (European Ferries)
— ZEEBRUGGE (European Ferries)

HARWICH — HOEK VAN HOLLAND (Sealink)
PARKESTON — OOSTENDE (Sealink)
QUAY — ESTBERG (DFDS)
— KRISTIANSAND (Fred Olsen)

HARWICH — BREMERHAVEN (Prins Ferries)
TOWN — HAMBURG (Prins Ferries)
— ZEEBRUGGE (Train Ferry)
— DUNKERQUE (Train Ferry)

Gogarth

Dovey
Junction

Abertafol

Aberdovey

Penhelig

Borth

35

VR

Glanrafon

Aberystwyth

Llanbadarn

Aberffrwd (Block Post)

Rheidol Falls

B

Capel Bangor

Rhiwfron

Nantyronen

Devil's
Bridge

VALE OF RHEIDOL (1' 11½")

C

0   5   10 m.   (1:350,000)
0   5   10   15 km.

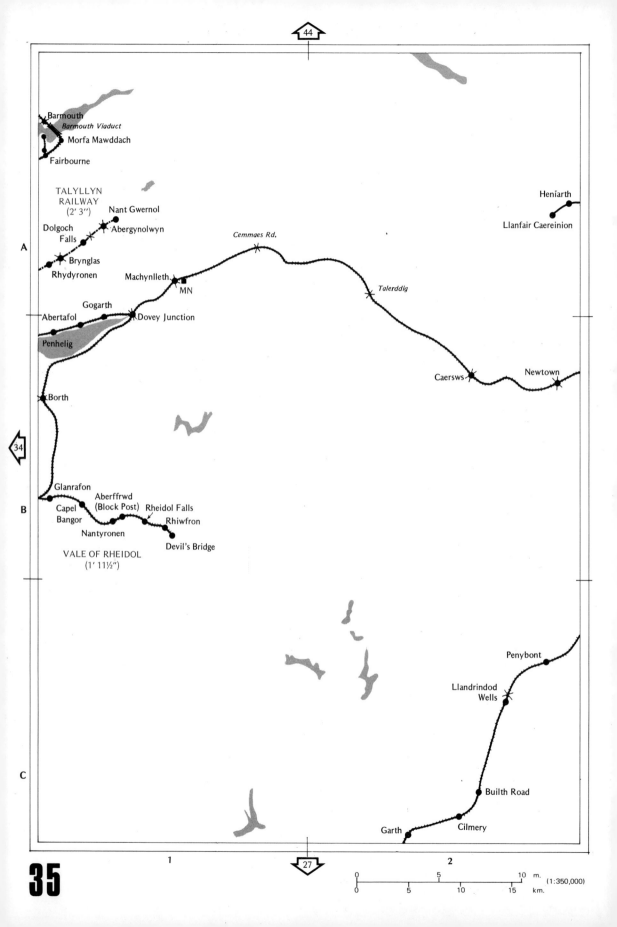

Barmouth
Barmouth Viaduct
Morfa Mawddach
Fairbourne

TALYLLYN
RAILWAY
(2' 3")

Nant Gwernol
Dolgoch
Falls
Abergynolwyn
Brynglas
Rhydyronen

Cemmaes Rd.

Machynlleth
MN

Heniarth
Llanfair Caereinion

A

Talerddig

Gogarth
Abertafol
Dovey Junction

Penhelig

Caersws
Newtown

Borth

Glanrafon
Aberffrwd
(Block Post)
Capel
Bangor
Rheidol Falls
Rhiwfron
Nantyronen
Devil's Bridge

VALE OF RHEIDOL
(1' 11½")

B

Penybont

Llandrindod
Wells

C

Builth Road

Garth
Cilmery

35

1
2

0   5   10 m.

0   5   10   15 km.

(1:350,000)

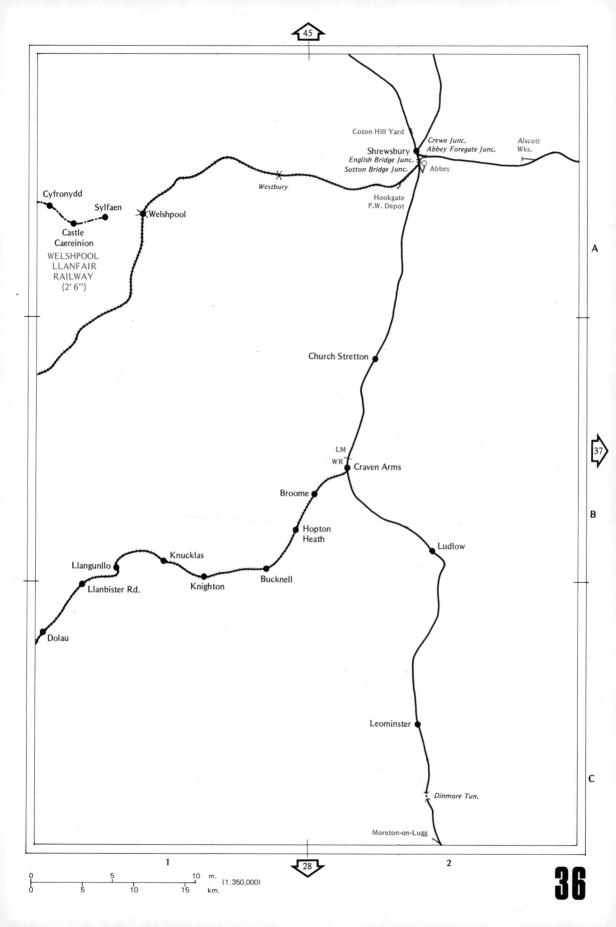

Coton Hill Yard

Crewe Junc.
Abbey Foregate Junc.

Alscott
Wks.

Shrewsbury
English Bridge Junc.
Sutton Bridge Junc.

Abbey

Cyfronydd

Sylfaen

Westbury

Welshpool

Hookgate
P.W. Depot

Castle
Caereinion

WELSHPOOL
LLANFAIR
RAILWAY
(2' 6")

A

Church Stretton

37

LM

WR

Craven Arms

Broome

B

Hopton
Heath

Ludlow

Knucklas

Llangunllo

Knighton

Bucknell

Llanbister Rd.

Dolau

Leominster

C

Dinmore Tun.

Moreton-on-Lugg

0 ────── 5 ────── 10 m.
0 ── 5 ── 10 ── 15 km.   (1:350,000)

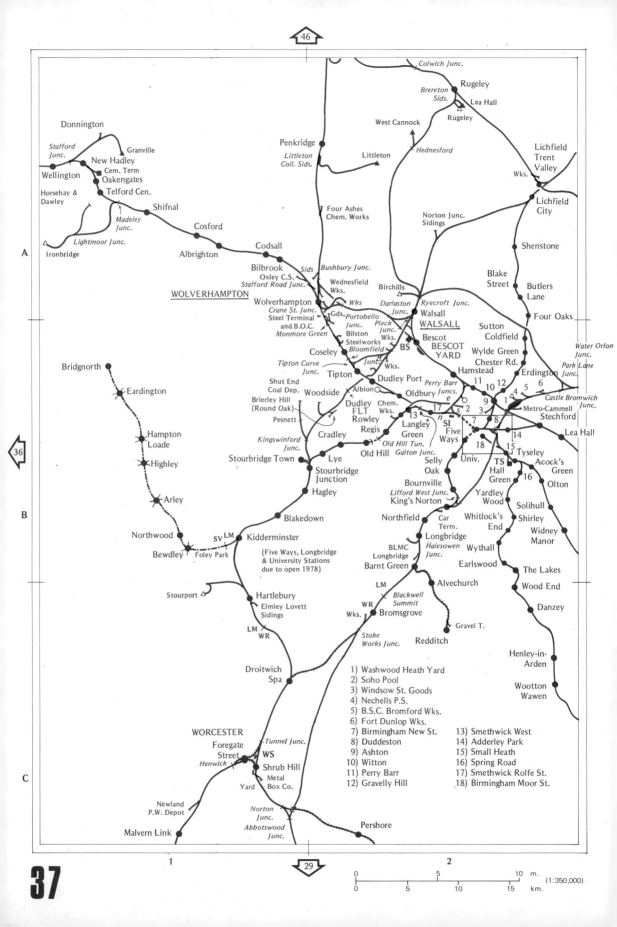

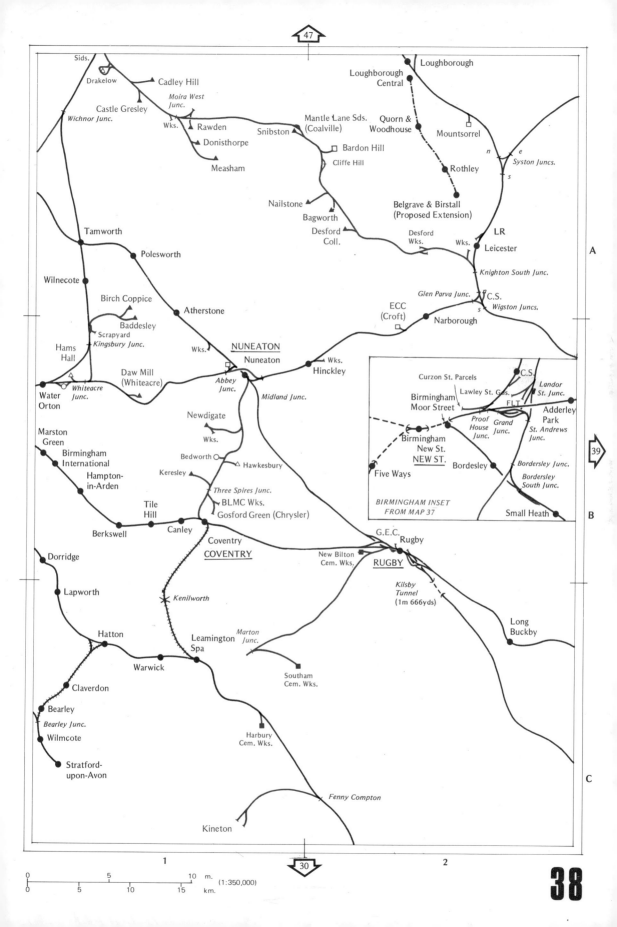

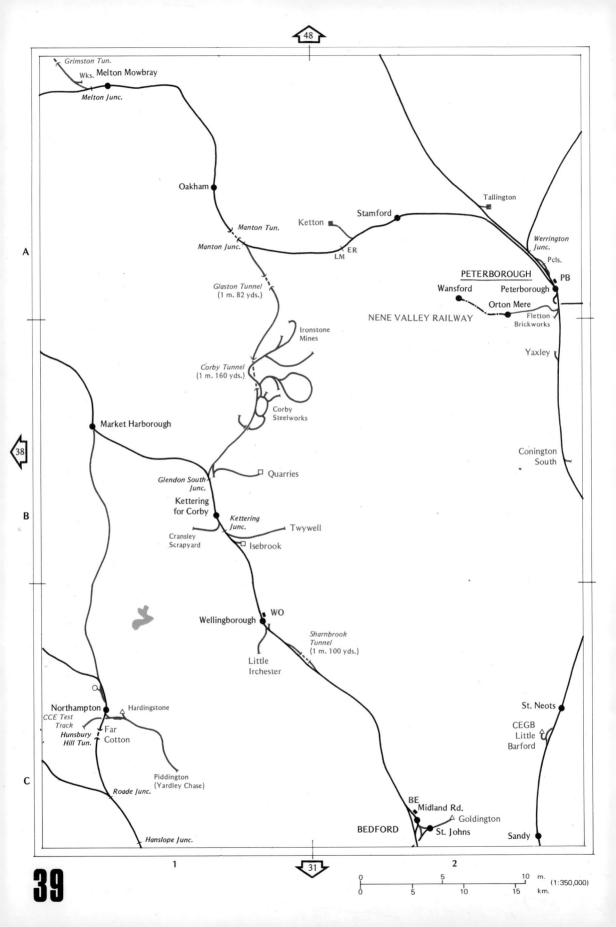

48

Grimston Tun.
Wks. Melton Mowbray
Melton Junc.

Oakham

Manton Tun.
Manton Junc.

Ketton
Stamford
Tallington

ER
LM

Glaston Tunnel
(1 m. 82 yds.)

PETERBOROUGH
Wansford   Peterborough
Orton Mere
NENE VALLEY RAILWAY

Werrington Junc.
Pcls.
PB

Fletton Brickworks

Yaxley

A

Ironstone Mines

Corby Tunnel
(1 m. 160 yds.)

Market Harborough

Corby Steelworks

Conington South

38

Glendon South Junc.

Quarries

Kettering for Corby
Kettering Junc.   Twywell

Cransley Scrapyard   Isebrook

B

WO
Wellingborough

Little Irchester

Sharnbrook Tunnel
(1 m. 100 yds.)

St. Neots

CEGB Little Barford

Northampton
CCE Test Track
Hardingstone
Hunsbury Hill Tun.   Far Cotton

Piddington (Yardley Chase)

Roade Junc.

BE
Midland Rd.
Goldington

BEDFORD   St. Johns

Sandy

C

Hanslope Junc.

1

31

2

0   5   10 m.
0   5   10   15 km.

(1:350,000)

39

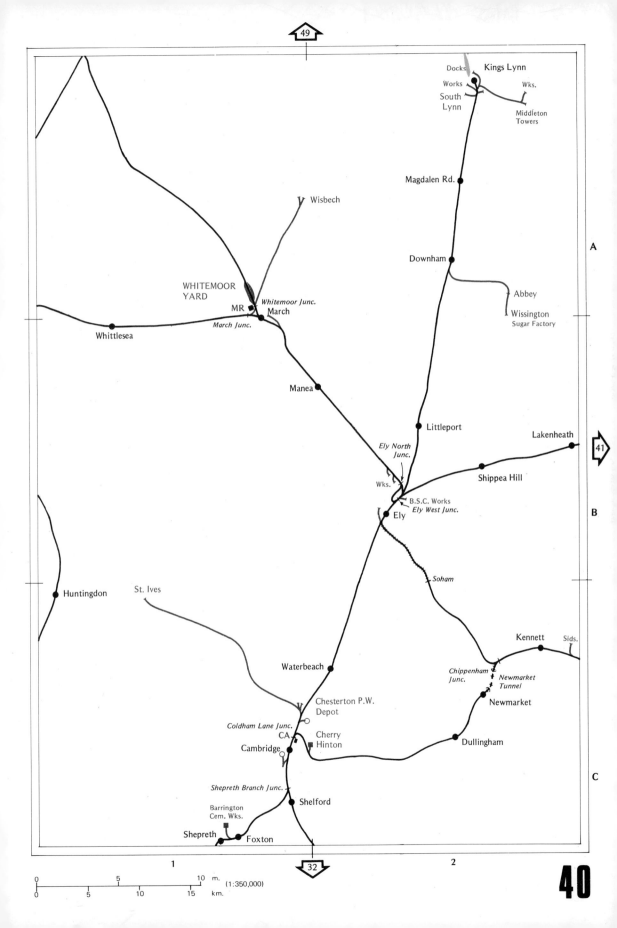

Docks Kings Lynn
Works Wks.
South
Lynn Middleton
Towers

Magdalen Rd.

Wisbech

Downham

WHITEMOOR
YARD

MR *Whitemoor Junc.* Abbey
March
March Junc. Wissington
Sugar Factory

Whittlesea

Manea

Littleport Lakenheath

*Ely North
Junc.*

Wks. Shippea Hill

B.S.C. Works
Ely West Junc.

Ely

St. Ives *Soham*

Huntingdon

Kennett Sids.

Waterbeach *Chippenham
Junc.* *Newmarket
Tunnel*

Chesterton P.W.
Depot Newmarket

Coldham Lane Junc.

CA Cherry
Hinton Dullingham

Cambridge

Shepreth Branch Junc.

Barrington Shelford
Cem. Wks.

Shepreth Foxton

A

B

C

1 2

0   5   10 m.   (1:350,000)
0   5   10   15 km.

40

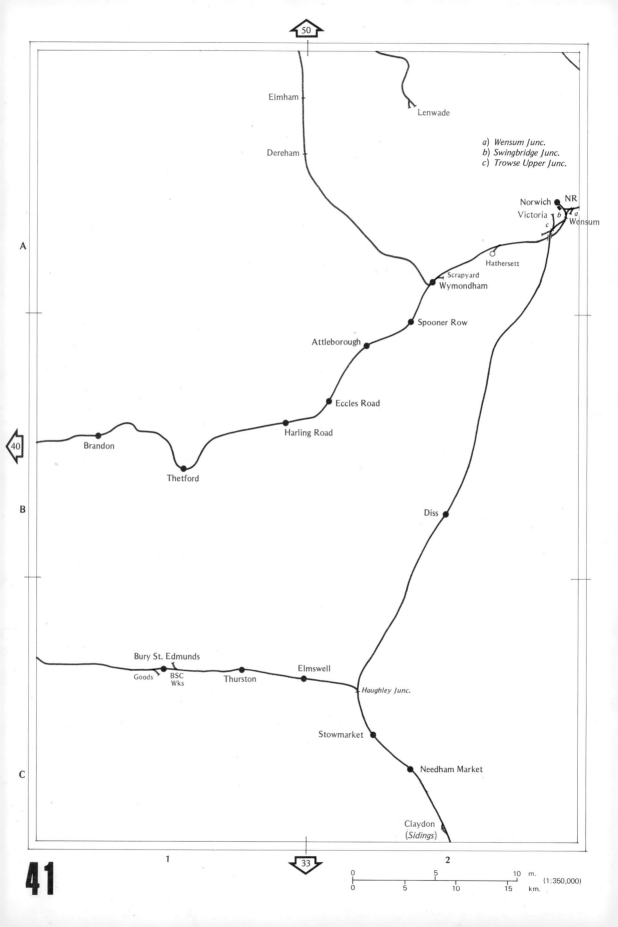

50

Elmham

Lenwade

Dereham

a) Wensum Junc.
b) Swingbridge Junc.
c) Trowse Upper Junc.

Norwich   NR
Victoria   *b*
         c   *a*
              Wensum

A

Hathersett

Scrapyard
Wymondham

Spooner Row

Attleborough

Eccles Road

Harling Road

Brandon

40

Thetford

B

Diss

Bury St. Edmunds

Goods   BSC
         Wks   Thurston

Elmswell

Haughley Junc.

Stowmarket

Needham Market

C

Claydon
(*Sidings*)

1

33

2

0 ____ 5 ____ 10 m.

0 __ 5 __ 10 __ 15 km.

(1:350,000)

41

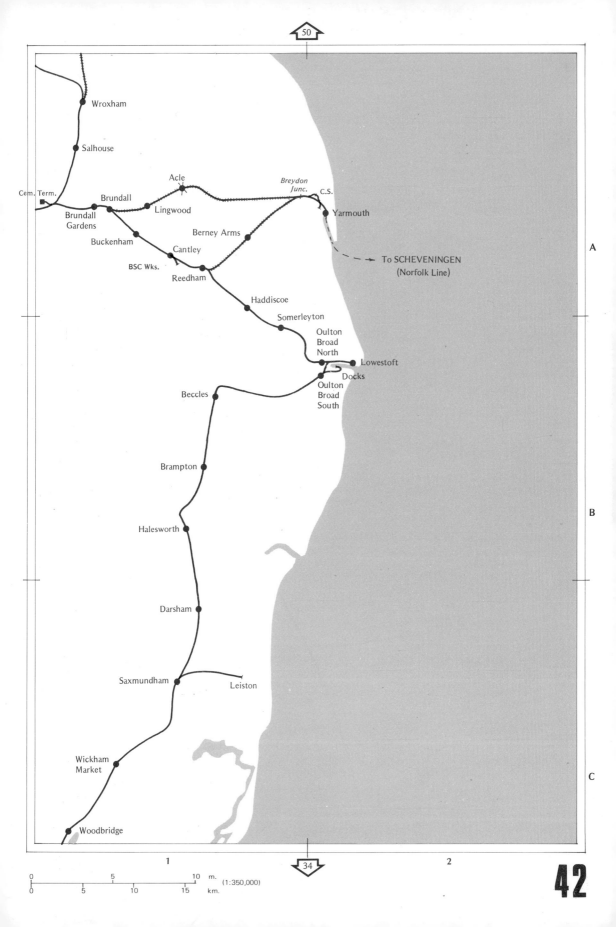

50

Wroxham

Salhouse

Acle

Breydon Junc.

C.S.

Cem. Term.

Brundall

Lingwood

Yarmouth

Brundall
Gardens

Buckenham

Berney Arms

A

Cantley

To SCHEVENINGEN
(Norfolk Line)

BSC Wks.

Reedham

Haddiscoe

Somerleyton

Oulton
Broad
North

Lowestoft

Docks

Beccles

Oulton
Broad
South

Brampton

Halesworth

B

Darsham

Saxmundham

Leiston

Wickham
Market

C

Woodbridge

1

34

2

0   5   10   m.   (1:350,000)
0   5   10   15   km.

42

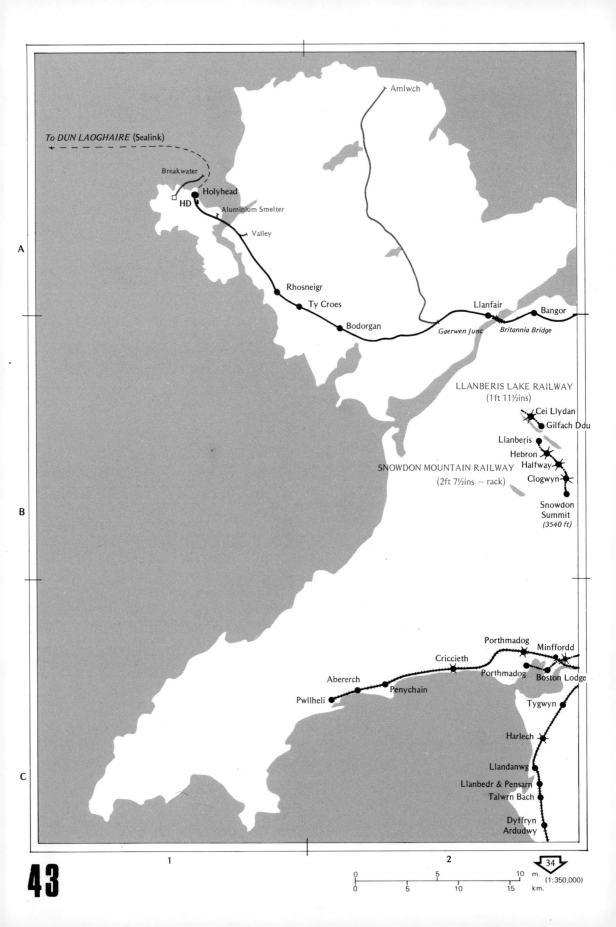

To DUN LAOGHAIRE (Sealink)

Breakwater

Holyhead
HD

Aluminium Smelter

Valley

Amlwch

Rhosneigr

Ty Croes

Bodorgan

Llanfair

Bangor

Gaerwen Junc

Britannia Bridge

LLANBERIS LAKE RAILWAY
(1ft 11½ins)

Cei Llydan
Gilfach Ddu

Llanberis
Hebron
Halfway

SNOWDON MOUNTAIN RAILWAY
(2ft 7½ins — rack)

Clogwyn

Snowdon
Summit
(3540 ft)

A

B

C

Porthmadog
Minffordd

Criccieth

Porthmadog
Boston Lodge

Abererch

Tygwyn

Penychain

Pwllheli

Harlech

Llandanwg

Llanbedr & Pensarn

Talwrn Bach

Dyffryn
Ardudwy

1

2

34
(1:350,000)

0   5   10
m.

0   5   10   15
km.

43

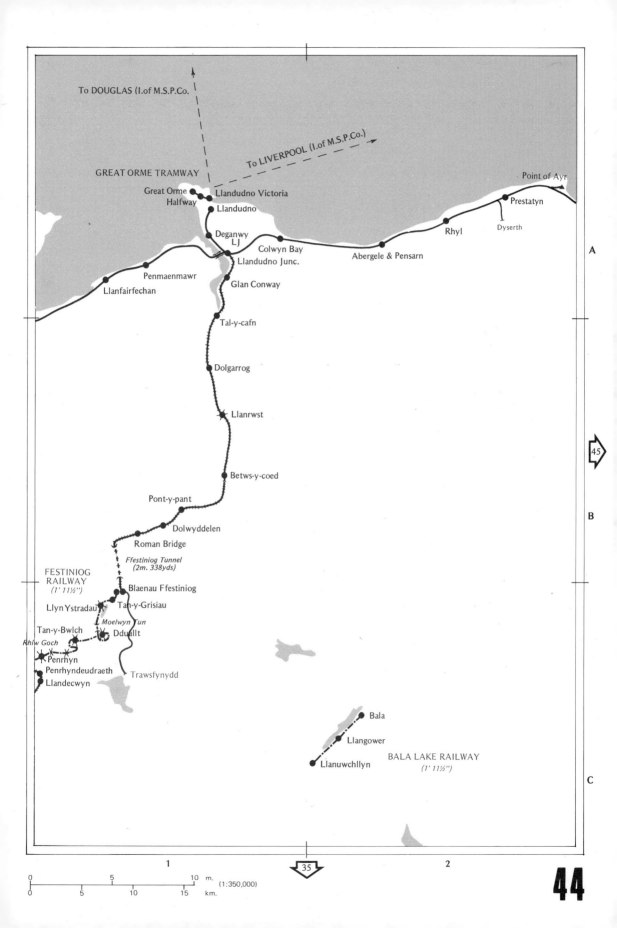

To DOUGLAS (I.of M.S.P.Co.)

To LIVERPOOL (I.of M.S.P.Co.)

GREAT ORME TRAMWAY

Point of Ayr

Great Orme
Halfway

Llandudno Victoria

Prestatyn

Llandudno

Deganwy
LJ

Rhyl

Dyserth

Colwyn Bay

Llandudno Junc.

Abergele & Pensarn

Penmaenmawr

Llanfairfechan

Glan Conway

Tal-y-cafn

Dolgarrog

Llanrwst

45

Betws-y-coed

Pont-y-pant

B

Dolwyddelen

Roman Bridge

FESTINIOG
RAILWAY
(1' 11½")

Ffestiniog Tunnel
(2m. 338yds)

Blaenau Ffestiniog

Llyn Ystradau

Tan-y-Grisiau

Tan-y-Bwlch

Moelwyn Tun

Rhiw Goch

Dduallt

Penrhyn

Penrhyndeudraeth

Trawsfynydd

Llandecwyn

Bala

Llangower

BALA LAKE RAILWAY
(1' 11½")

Llanuwchllyn

C

1

35

2

A

```
0        5        10  m.   (1:350,000)
0    5    10    15  km.
```

44

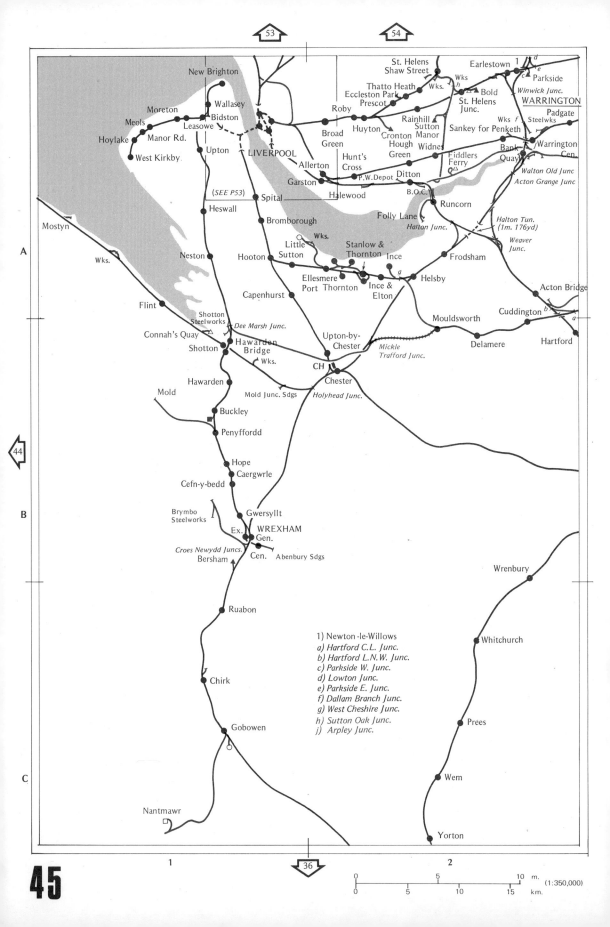

New Brighton

Moreton
Wallasey
Meols
Bidston
Hoylake
Leasowe
Manor Rd.
West Kirkby
Upton
LIVERPOOL
Spital
(SEE P53)
Heswall
Bromborough
Mostyn
Neston
Little
Sutton
Stanlow &
Thornton
Ince
Wks.
Hooton
Ellesmere
Port
Thornton
Ince &
Elton
Frodsham
Helsby
Flint
Capenhurst
Shotton
Steelworks
Dee Marsh Junc.
Connah's Quay
Hawarden
Bridge
Upton-by-
Chester
Mickle
Trafford Junc.
Mouldsworth
Cuddington
Shotton
Wks.
Acton Bridge
Hartford
Delamere
Hawarden
CH
Mold
Chester
Mold Junc. Sdgs
Holyhead Junc.
Buckley
Penyffordd
Hope
Caergwrle
Cefn-y-bedd
Brymbo
Steelworks
Gwersyllt
Ex.
WREXHAM
Gen.
Croes Newydd Juncs.
Bersham
Cen.
Abenbury Sdgs
Wrenbury
Ruabon
Whitchurch
Chirk
Prees
Gobowen
Wem
Nantmawr
Yorton

St. Helens
Shaw Street
Earlestown
Parkside
Thatto Heath
Wks.
Bold
Eccleston Park
Prescot
St. Helens
Junc.
Winwick Junc.
Roby
Rainhill
Sutton
Manor
Sankey for Penketh
WARRINGTON
Padgate
Steelwks
Huyton
Cronton
Widnes
Broad
Green
Hough
Green
Wks.
Hunt's
Cross
Bank
Quay
Warrington
Cen.
Allerton
Fiddlers
Ferry
Walton Old Junc
Garston
P.W.Depot
Ditton
Acton Grange Junc
Halewood
B.O.C.
Runcorn
Folly Lane
Halton Junc.
Halton Tun.
(1m. 176yd)
Weaver
Junc.

1) Newton -le-Willows
a) Hartford C.L. Junc.
b) Hartford L.N.W. Junc.
c) Parkside W. Junc.
d) Lowton Junc.
e) Parkside E. Junc.
f) Dallam Branch Junc.
g) West Cheshire Junc.
h) Sutton Oak Junc.
j) Arpley Junc.

A

44

B

C

1   2

36

0   5   10 m.   (1:350,000)
0   5   10   15 km.

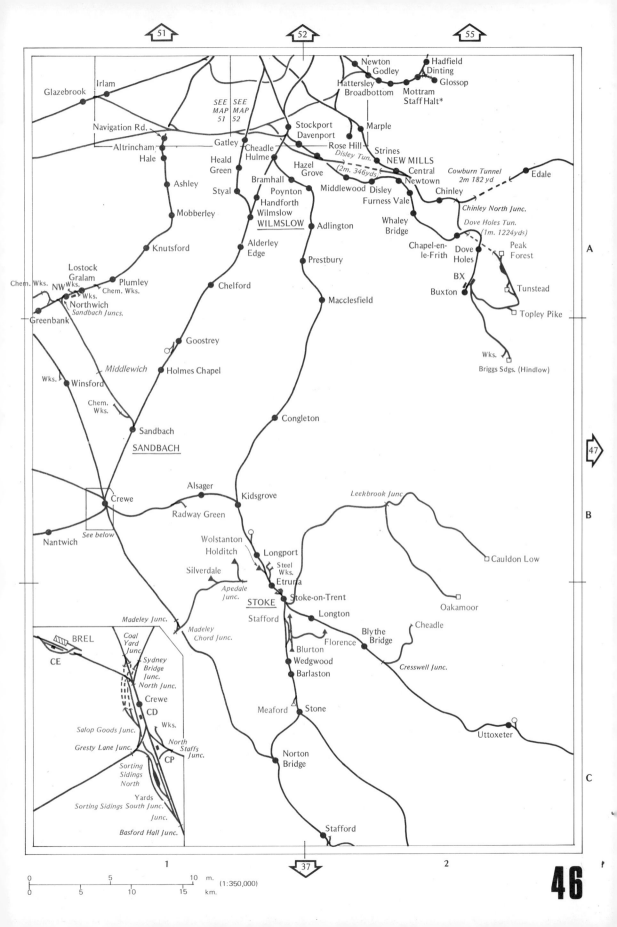

Chapeltown
Oughtibridge
New Stubbin
Chapeltown
Wks.
Thryburgh Junc.
Aldwarke Junc.
Rotherham
Silverwood
Maltby
Firbeck Juncs.
Harworth
Wincobank
Stn. Junc.
Wadsley
Bridge*
Brightside
Brightside
Junc.
Masborough S. Junc.
Wks
Wks.
Attercliffe
TINSLEY
YARD
Thurcroft
DA Wks.
TI
Treeton Juncs.
Treeton
Dinnington
Sheffield
Darnall
Woodhouse
Orgreave
Dinnington
Station Junc.
SHEFFIELD
Nunnery Junc.
Beighton
Kiveton
Bridge
Kiveton
Park
Brancliffe E. Junc.
Shireoaks Stn. Junc.
Rotherwood Yard
Beighton Stn. Junc.
Beighton
Junc.
Kiveton
Park
Shireoaks
Shireoaks E. Junc.
Worksop
Hope
Bamford
Hathersage
Dore
LM
ER
Bradway Tun.(1m. 267yds)
Westthorpe
(Spink Hill)
Shireoaks
Steetley
Woodend
Junc.
Manton Wood
Cem. Wks.
Totley Tun.
Grindleford (3m. 950yds)
Renishaw Park
Foxlow Junc.
BH
Hall Lane Junc.
Ireland
Seymour Junc.
Whitwell
Elmton & Cresswell Junc.
A
Scrapyard
Staveley
Wks
Tapton
Junc.
Stanfree
Stanfree
Markham
Bolsover
Langwith
Warsop
Vale
Welbeck
Thoresby
Ollerton
Chesterfield
Arkwright
Town
Warsop Junc.
Shirebrook
SB
Clipstone
Junc.
Boughton
Junc.
ER
LM
Avenue Carbonisation
Clay Cross
Clay Cross Junc.
Glapwell
Pleasley ER
LM
Clipstone
Yard
Welbeck
Clay Cross Tun.(1m. 24yds)
Teversal
Sherwood
Mansfield
Bilsthorpe
Cowdor
Matlock
Matlock Bath
Cromford
High Tor Tuns.
Morton
Blackwell
Juncs.
WT
Mansfield S.
Junc.
Sutton
New
Hucknall
Sutton in
Ashfield
ER
LM
Rufford
Blidworth
Wirksworth
TRAMWAY
MUSEUM SOC.
Cliffe Quarry
Crich
Alfreton &
Mansfield
Parkway
Bentinck
B
Whatstandwell
Ambergate
Ripley
Pye Bridge
Junc.
Pye Hill
Annesley
Newstead
Linby
Hucknall
Calverton
Belper
Denby
Moor Green
Bestwood Park Junc.
Bestwood
Lowdham
Duffield
Gedling
Burton
Joyce
Carlton
Netherfield
Radcliffe
Little Eaton Junc.
Wks.
Radford
Junc.
Trowell
Junc.
Nottingham
Mickleover
DERBY
BREL
Chaddesden
C.S. Spondon
Stanton Wks.
Lenton Juncs.
TO
FLT
NM
Colwick
Steel Wks
North Wilford
(Test Track)
Derby
DY
Peartree
Melbourne Junc.
Sinfin N.
Sinfin Cen.
Wks.
Spondon
Chilwell
TOTON
YARD
Wks.
Beeston
Edwalton
Cotgrave
Stenson N. Staffs
Junc.
Stenson Junc.
Wks.
Gravel Pits
Sheet Stores Junc.
Long
Eaton
Attenborough
TRENT
Ruddington
C
Tutbury
Eggington Junc.
Willington
Worthington Junc.
Trent Juncs.
Ratcliffe
Hotchley Hill
Stanton Tun.
Leicester Junc.
Burton-on-Trent
Branston Junc.
Birmingham Curve Junc.
Castle
Donington
East Leake
(Test Track)
Worthington

1
38
2
0 5 10 m.
0 5 10 15 km.
(1:350,000)
46

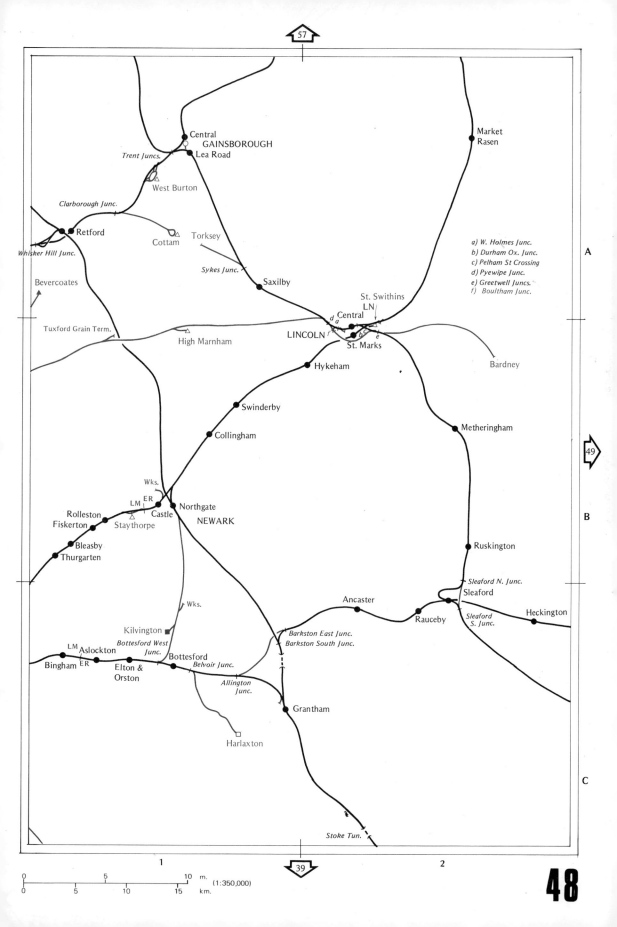

Central
GAINSBOROUGH
Lea Road
Trent Juncs.
West Burton
Clarborough Junc.
Retford
Cottam
Torksey
Whisker Hill Junc.
Bevercoates
Sykes Junc.
Saxilby
St. Swithins
LN
d Central
a
LINCOLN
St. Marks
f
b *c*
e
Tuxford Grain Term.
High Marnham
Bardney
Hykeham

a) W. Holmes Junc.
b) Durham Ox. Junc.
c) Pelham St Crossing
d) Pyewipe Junc.
e) Greetwell Juncs.
f) Boultham Junc.

Swinderby
Collingham
Metheringham

Wks.
LM ER
Rolleston
Fiskerton
Staythorpe
Castle
Northgate
NEWARK
Ruskington

Bleasby
Thurgarten

Sleaford N. Junc.
Sleaford
Ancaster
Sleaford
S. Junc.
Heckington
Rauceby

Wks.
Kilvington
Bottesford West Junc.
Bottesford
Belvoir Junc.
Barkston East Junc.
Barkston South Junc.
LM Aslockton
Bingham ER
Elton &
Orston
Allington Junc.
Grantham
Harlaxton

Stoke Tun.

1

2

0   5   10 m.
          (1:350,000)
0   5   10   15 km.

48

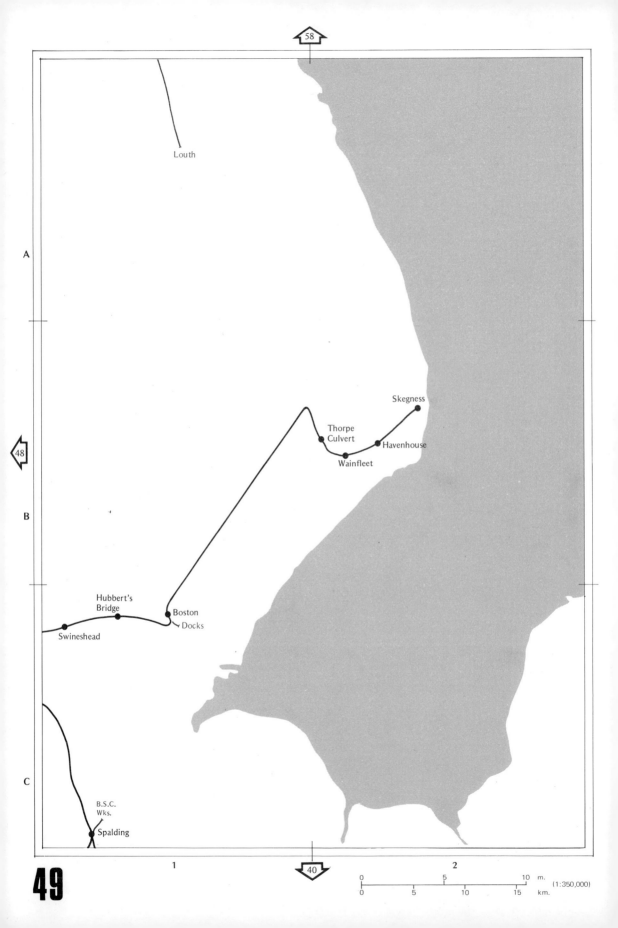

58

Louth

A

48

Skegness

Thorpe
Culvert
Havenhouse

Wainfleet

B

Hubbert's
Bridge   Boston
                  Docks
Swineshead

C

B.S.C.
Wks.
Spalding

49

1   40   2

0   5   10 m.
0   5   10   15 km.   (1:350,000)

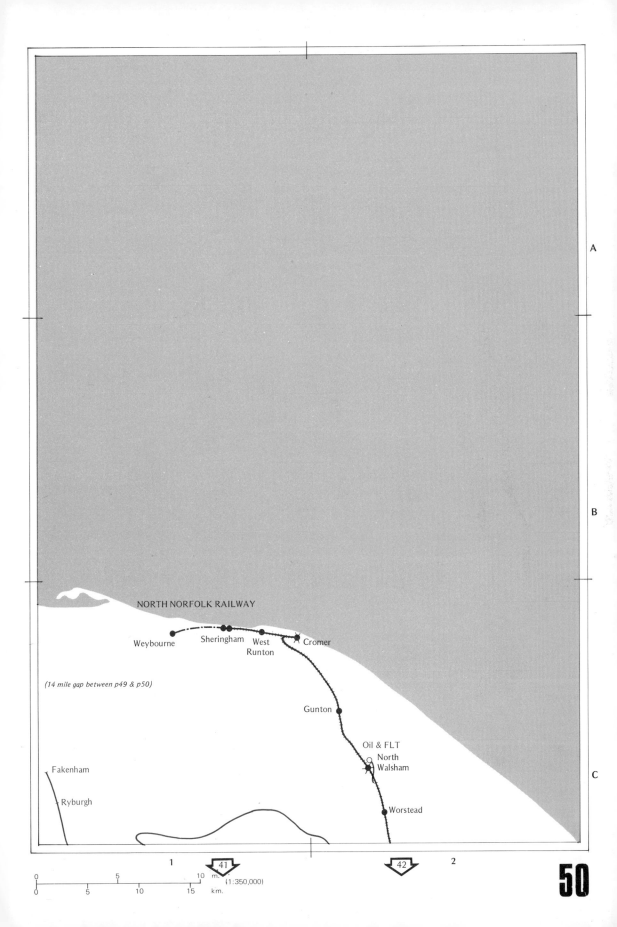

NORTH NORFOLK RAILWAY

Weybourne   Sheringham   West   Cromer
                           Runton

(14 mile gap between p49 & p50)

Gunton

Oil & FLT
North
Walsham

Fakenham

Ryburgh   Worstead

1   41   42   2

0   5   10 m.
                        (1:350,000)
0   5   10   15 km.

50

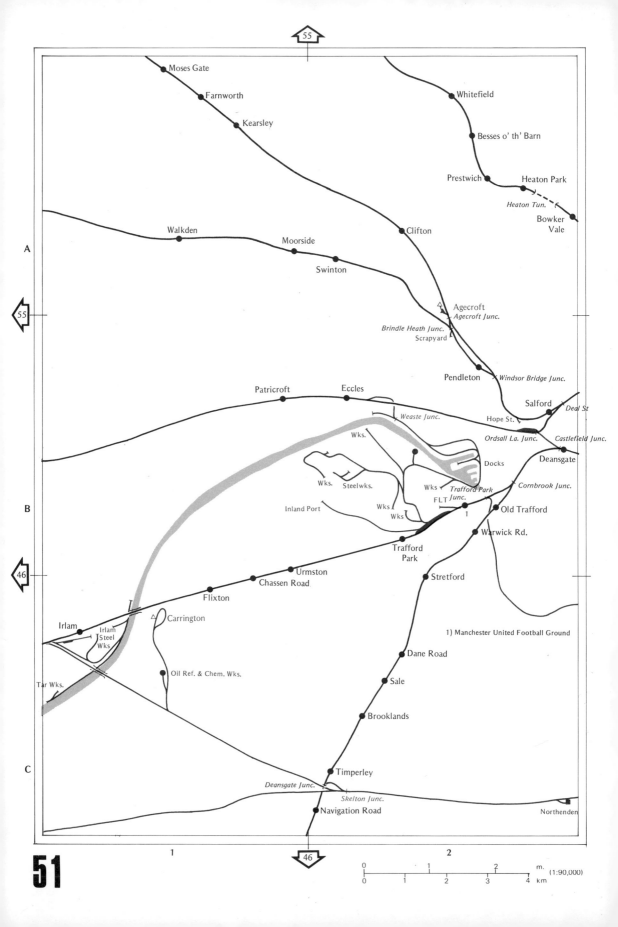

Moses Gate

Farnworth

Kearsley

Whitefield

Besses o' th' Barn

Prestwich   Heaton Park

Heaton Tun.

Bowker
Vale

Walkden

Moorside   Clifton

Swinton

△ Agecroft
Agecroft Junc.

Brindle Heath Junc.
Scrapyard

Pendleton   × *Windsor Bridge Junc.*

Patricroft   Eccles   Salford   *Deal St*

Weaste Junc.   Hope St.

Ordsall La. Junc.   *Castlefield Junc.*

Wks.   Docks   Deansgate

B

Wks.   *Cornbrook Junc.*

Wks.   Steelwks.   Wks   *Trafford Park*
                                 Junc.
Inland Port   Wks   FLT   Old Trafford
                         Wks   1
                                              Warwick Rd.

Trafford
Park   Stretford

Urmston
Chassen Road.

Flixton

Irlam   △ Carrington
Irlam
Steel
Wks   1) Manchester United Football Ground

Oil Ref. & Chem. Wks.   Dane Road

Tar Wks.   Sale

Brooklands

C

Timperley

Deansgate Junc.

Skelton Junc.
Navigation Road   Northenden

1   46   2

0   1   2   m. (1:90,000)
0   1   2   3   4 km

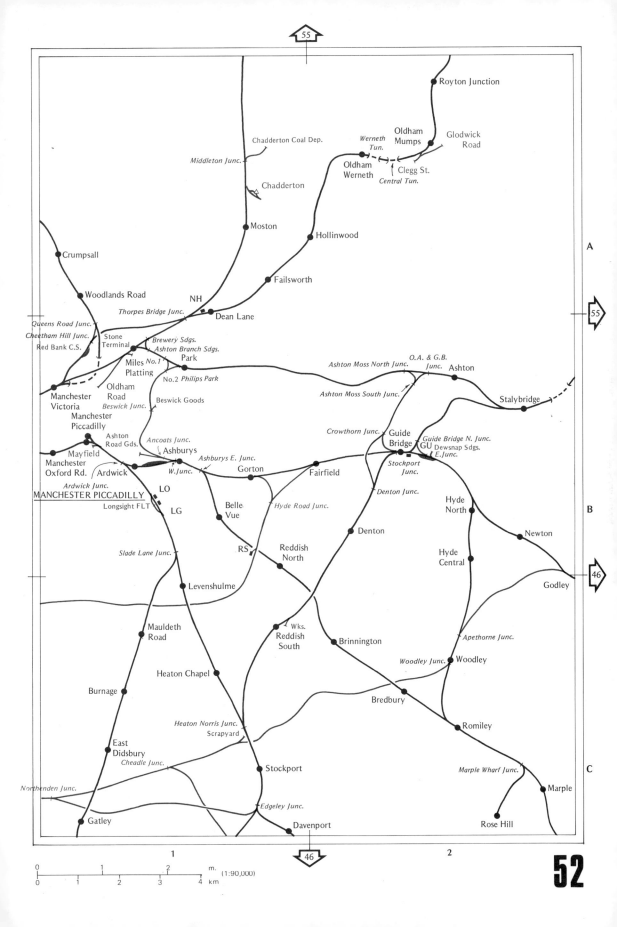

Royton Junction

Chadderton Coal Dep.

Werneth
Tun.

Oldham
Mumps

Glodwick
Road

Middleton Junc.

Oldham
Werneth

Clegg St.

Central Tun.

Chadderton

Moston

Hollinwood

Crumpsall

Failsworth

Woodlands Road

NH

Thorpes Bridge Junc.

Dean Lane

Queens Road Junc.

Cheetham Hill Junc.

Red Bank C.S.

Stone
Terminal

Brewery Sdgs.

Ashton Branch Sdgs.

Park

Miles
Platting

No.1

No.2 Philips Park

O.A. & G.B.
Junc.

Ashton

Ashton Moss North Junc.

Manchester
Victoria

Oldham
Road

Beswick Junc.

Beswick Goods

Ashton Moss South Junc.

Stalybridge

Manchester
Piccadilly

Ashton
Road Gds.

Ancoats Junc.

Ashburys

Crowthorn Junc.

Guide
Bridge

GU

Guide Bridge N. Junc.

Dewsnap Sdgs.

Mayfield

Ashburys E. Junc.

E.Junc.

Manchester
Oxford Rd.

Ardwick

W.Junc.

Gorton

Fairfield

Stockport
Junc.

Ardwick Junc.

LO

Denton Junc.

Hyde
North

MANCHESTER PICCADILLY

Longsight FLT

LG

Belle
Vue

Hyde Road Junc.

Denton

Newton

Slade Lane Junc.

RS

Reddish
North

Hyde
Central

Levenshulme

Godley

Mauldeth
Road

Wks.

Reddish
South

Brinnington

Apethorne Junc.

Heaton Chapel

Woodley Junc.

Woodley

Burnage

Bredbury

Heaton Norris Junc.

Scrapyard

Romiley

East
Didsbury

Cheadle Junc.

Stockport

Marple Wharf Junc.

Northenden Junc.

Marple

Edgeley Junc.

Gatley

Davenport

Rose Hill

1

2

0   1   2   m.   (1:90,000)
0 1 2 3 4 km

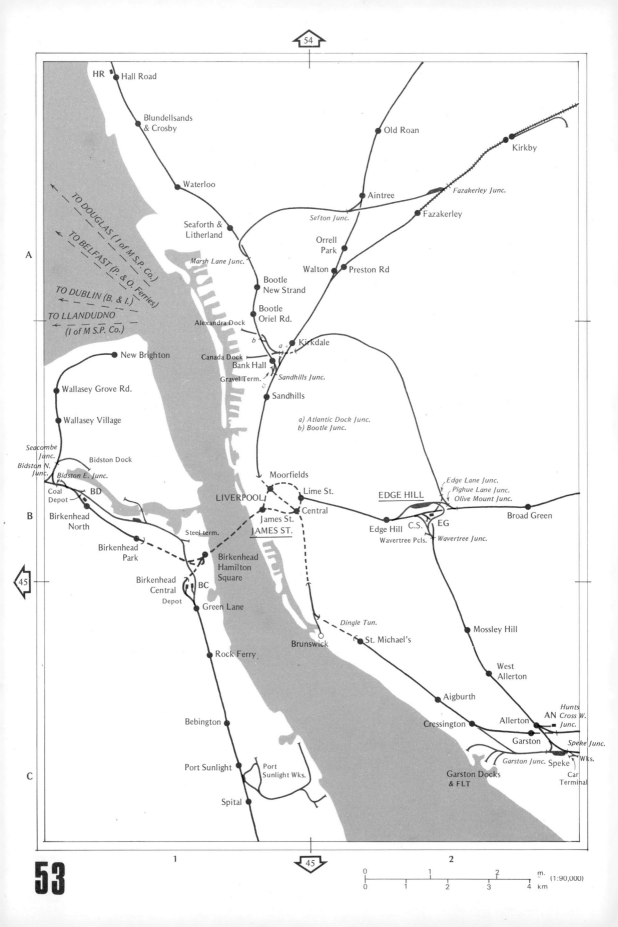

HR Hall Road

Blundellsands
& Crosby

Old Roan

Kirkby

Waterloo

Aintree

Fazakerley Junc.

Seaforth &
Litherland

Sefton Junc.

Fazakerley

TO DOUGLAS (I of M.S.P. Co.)

TO BELFAST (P. & O. Ferries)

TO DUBLIN (B. & I.)

TO LLANDUDNO (I of M.S.P. Co.)

Orrell
Park

Walton

Preston Rd

A

Marsh Lane Junc.

Bootle
New Strand

Bootle
Oriel Rd.

Alexandra Dock

b   a   Kirkdale

New Brighton

Canada Dock
Bank Hall

Gravel Term.

Sandhills Junc.

Wallasey Grove Rd.

Sandhills

Wallasey Village

a) Atlantic Dock Junc.
b) Bootle Junc.

*Seacombe
Junc.*
*Bidston N.
Junc.*

Bidston Dock

Bidston E. Junc.

Coal
Depot   BD

Birkenhead
North

Moorfields

Lime St.

EDGE HILL

Edge Lane Junc.
Pighue Lane Junc.
Olive Mount Junc.

Broad Green

B

LIVERPOOL

Central

Steel term.

James St.
JAMES ST.

Edge Hill

C.S.

EG

Wavertree Pcls.

Wavertree Junc.

Birkenhead
Park

Birkenhead
Hamilton
Square

Birkenhead
Central
Depot   BC

45

Green Lane

Dingle Tun.

Brunswick

St. Michael's

Mossley Hill

Rock Ferry

West
Allerton

Aigburth

*Hunts
Cross W.
Junc.*

Bebington

Cressington

Allerton   AN

Garston

Speke Junc.

Port Sunlight

Port
Sunlight Wks.

Garston Junc. Speke

Wks.

C

Garston Docks
& FLT

Car
Terminal

Spital

1   45   2

0   1   2   m.
                         (1:90,000)
0   1   2   3   4 km

Steelwks. Barrow Roose
BW Roose

Wennington

Bare Lane *Hest Bank*
Morecambe *Morecambe South Junc.*
Chem. Wks. Lancaster

Heysham Harbour

Chem. Wks.

TO DOUGLAS (I of M S.P. Co.)

A

Fleetwood ● Knott End
Ash St.
△ Fleetwood
Rossall
Thornton Gate
Cleveleys
Little Bispham
Burn Naze
BLACKPOOL & FLEETWOOD Bispham
TRAMWAYS *(PRINCIPAL STOPS)* Cabin
C.S. Poulton-le-Fylde
Layton
Talbot Sq. Blackpool North
Tower
Manchester Sq. Kirkham & Wesham
Depot
Pleasure Beach Blackpool South Salwick
Starr Gate Squires Gate Wks.
St. Annes Maudlands
Red Scar
Strand Road Deepdale Coal Dep.
(Docks) Preston
Ansdell & Fairhaven Lytham Penwortham
PRESTON Pleasington
Farington Curve Junc.
B
a) Lostock Hall Junc. *a* Bamber Bridge
b) Ince Moss Junc. *Farington Junc.* BLMC
c) Springs Branch Junc. Wks. Leyland
d) Bamfurlong Junc.
e) Golborne Stn. Junc. *Euxton Junc.*
b) Ince Moss Junc. Croston
Chorley
Coal Depot Meols Cop
Southport Rufford Adlington
C.S. Bescar Lane Burscough Bridge
Birkdale New Lane Hoscar Blackrod Horwich
Hillside Burscough Junc. Parbold BREL
Ainsdale Appley Bridge
1) Ashton-in-Makerfield* Ormskirk Gathurst Wks. **WIGAN**
2) Bickershaw Coll. Freshfield Aughton Park Hindley
3) Golborne Formby Town Green Upholland Orrell Wallgate Ince
4) Coop Glassworks N.W. *c* SP *Crow Nest Junc.*
Hightown Pemberton 4
Maghull Rainford *b* *d*
Hall Road Bryn *e*
Old Roan Garswood 1
Kirkby Mill Lane 3 2
Haydock
Golborne Junc.
C

1 2
0 5 10 m.
0 5 10 15 km. (1:350,000)

53 45

54

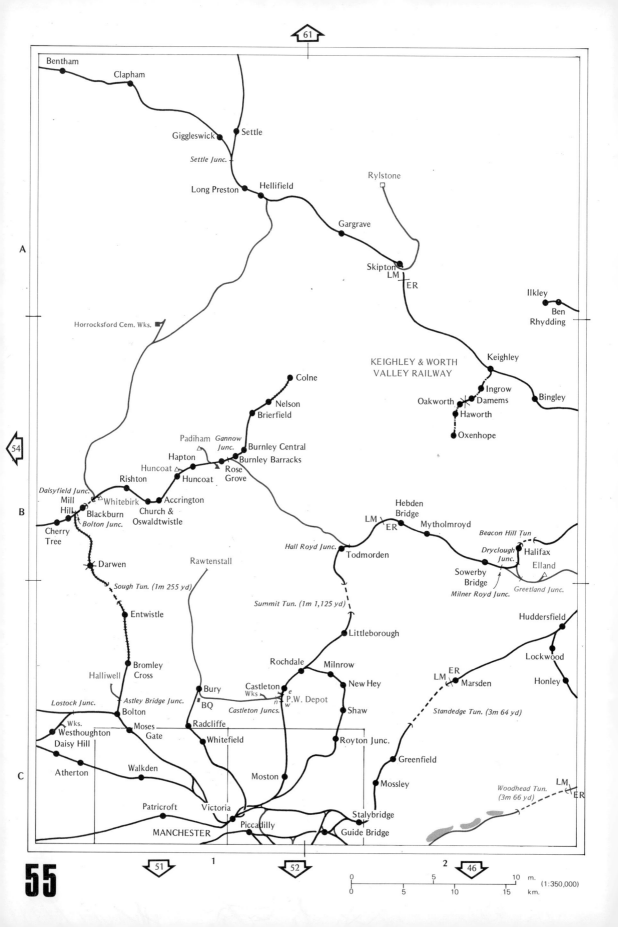

Bentham
Clapham
Giggleswick
Settle
Settle Junc.
Long Preston
Hellifield
Gargrave
Rylstone
Skipton
LM | ER

Ilkley
Ben Rhydding

A

Horrocksford Cem. Wks.

Keighley
KEIGHLEY & WORTH VALLEY RAILWAY
Ingrow
Oakworth
Damems
Bingley
Haworth
Oxenhope

Colne
Nelson
Brierfield

Padiham
Gannow Junc.
Hapton
Burnley Central
Huncoat △
Burnley Barracks
Rishton
Huncoat
Rose Grove

Daisyfield Junc.
Mill Hill
Whitebirk △
Accrington
Church & Oswaldtwistle

Hebden Bridge
LM | ER
Mytholmroyd
Beacon Hill Tun
Dryclough Junc.
Halifax

B

Blackburn
Bolton Junc.
Cherry Tree
Hall Royd Junc.
Todmorden
Sowerby Bridge
Milner Royd Junc.
Elland
Greetland Junc.

Darwen

Sough Tun. (1m 255 yd)

Summit Tun. (1m 1,125 yd)

Huddersfield

Entwistle
Littleborough
Lockwood

Bromley Cross
Rochdale
Milnrow
LM | ER
Marsden
Honley

Halliwell
Bury
Castleton Wks.
New Hey
Standedge Tun. (3m 64 yd)

Lostock Junc.
Astley Bridge Junc.
BQ
e
P.W. Depot
n
w
Shaw

Bolton
Castleton Juncs.
Wks.
Westhoughton
Moses Gate
Radcliffe
Daisy Hill
Whitefield
Royton Junc.
Greenfield

C

Atherton
Walkden
Moston
Mossley
Woodhead Tun. (3m 66 yd)
LM | ER

Patricroft
Victoria
Stalybridge
MANCHESTER
Piccadilly
Guide Bridge

0   5   10 m.   (1:350,000)
0   5   10   15 km.

54

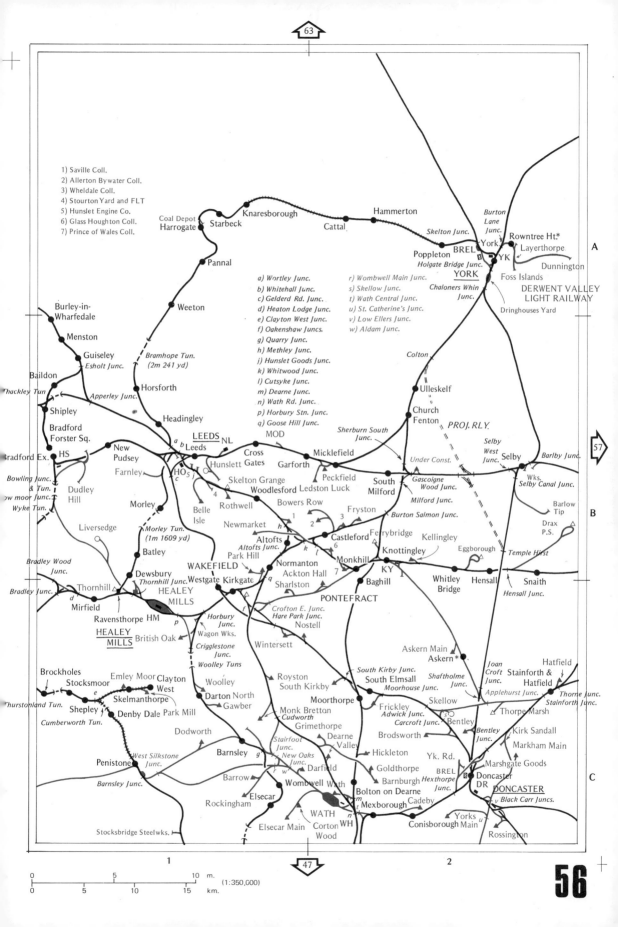

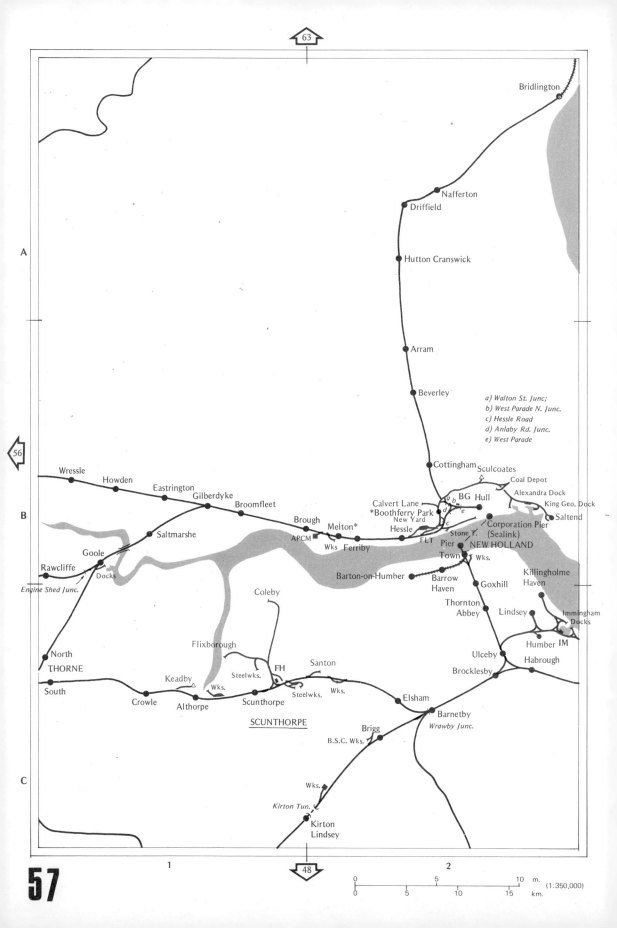

Bridlington

Nafferton
Driffield

A

Hutton Cranswick

Arram

Beverley

a) Walton St. Junc;
b) West Parade N. Junc.
c) Hessle Road
d) Anlaby Rd. Junc.
e) West Parade

Wressle
Howden
Eastrington
Gilberdyke
Broomfleet

Cottingham
Sculcoates
Coal Depot
Alexandra Dock
King Geo. Dock

Calvert Lane
*Boothferry Park
New Yard
Hessle

a b
d e
c

BG Hull

Saltend

B

Brough
Melton*
APCM
Wks. Ferriby

Stone T.
Corporation Pier
(Sealink)

FLT
Pier
Town

NEW HOLLAND

Wks.

Goole
Saltmarshe

Rawcliffe
Docks

Engine Shed Junc.

Barton-on-Humber
Barrow
Haven
Goxhill

Killingholme
Haven

Coleby

Thornton
Abbey
Lindsey

Immingham
Docks

Flixborough

Humber IM

North
THORNE

Keadby
Santon

Ulceby
Brocklesby

Habrough

South
Crowle
Althorpe

Steelwks.
FH

Wks.
Steelwks.

Wks.

Scunthorpe

Elsham

Barnetby
Wrawby Junc.

SCUNTHORPE

Brigg
B.S.C. Wks.

C

Wks.

Kirton Tun.

Kirton
Lindsey

1

2

0   5   10 m.
0   5   10   15 km.

(1:350,000)

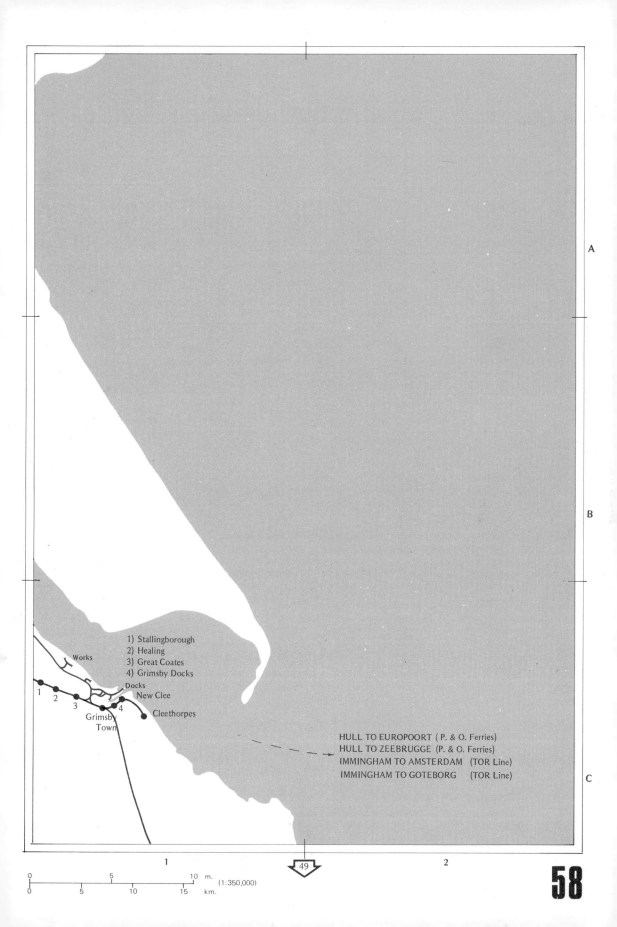

Works

1) Stallingborough
2) Healing
3) Great Coates
4) Grimsby Docks

Docks
New Clee

1 2 3 4 Cleethorpes

Grimsby
Town

HULL TO EUROPOORT (P. & O. Ferries)
HULL TO ZEEBRUGGE (P. & O. Ferries)
IMMINGHAM TO AMSTERDAM   (TOR Line)
IMMINGHAM TO GOTEBORG   (TOR Line)

A

B

C

1

49

2

0   5   10   m.   (1:350,000)
0   5   10   15   km.

58

A

Solway ▲ ● Maryport
● Flimby
Siddick Junc.
Broughton Moor
Workington
Steelworks
Calva Junc.
● Workington
WK
● Harrington

Siddick Junc.
Parton
Docks ● Whitehaven
Haig Coll. *Corkickle Tun*
Corkickle
□ Rowrah
Marchon Chem. Wks. *Mirehouse Junc.*
Moor Row
● St. Bees
Egremont
Nethertown ✳ Beckermet
● Braystones
Sellafield
Windscale
Seascale

B

Ramsey ●
Bellevue
Lewaigue
MANX ELECTRIC RAILWAY
(3FT 0 INS DERBY CASTLE - RAMSEY)
(3FT 6 INS LAXEY - SNAEFELL)
Cornaa
Dreemskerry
Ballaglass
Ballajora
Glen Mona
Drigg ● *Miteside* ✳
Ravenglass ● Muncaster Mill
Snaefell
Dhoon
Bungalow
Ballaragh
ISLE
OF MAN
Depot Minorca
Laxey
Fairy Cottage South
Ballabeg Cape
Garwick Glen
Baldrine
Eskmeals
Bootle ●
"TO BELFAST
"TO ARDROSSAN
Depot
Groudle Glen
DOUGLAS CORP. HORSETRAMS Derby Castle Howstrake
(3FT 0 INS PIER - DERBY CASTLE) Douglas Onchan Head
(All I of M Steam Packet Co.)
ISLE OF MAN STEAM RAILWAY Port Soderick
(3 FT 0 INS) Douglas Pier TO FLEETWOOD

C

Ballasalla
Port Erin ● TO LIVERPOOL
Port St. Mary ✳ Castletown
TO DUBLIN

TO LLANDUDNO

1   2

0   5   10 m.
| | | | | | | | (1:350,000)
0   5   10   15 km.

Aspatria

Lazonby*

Langwathby*

Penrith

Wks. A

Pooley Bridge

ULLSWATER

Howtown

Glenridding

Harrison's Limeworks □ Shap Summit (916ft)

61

Ambleside

Irton
Road
Dalegarth
Beckfoot
Eskdale
Green
RAVENGLASS & ESKDALE
RAILWAY (1' 3'')

B

Windermere
Staveley

Bowness

Burnside

Kendal

WINDERMERE

(SEALINK)

Oxenholme

LAKESIDE & HAVERTHWAITE
RAILWAY
Lakeside
Newby Bridge

Foxfield

Haverthwaite

Green Road

Silecroft

Kirkby-in
Furness

Millom

Plumpton Junc.
Ulverston

Wks.

Askam

Grange-over-
Sands

Cark &
Cartmel

Arnside

Waterslack □ Silverdale

C

Park South Junc.

Dalton
Dalton Junc.

Kents
Bank

East
Junc.

Furness & Midland Junc.
Carnforth Wks.

1

10 m. (1:350,000)

0   5
0   5   10   15 km.

54

2

60

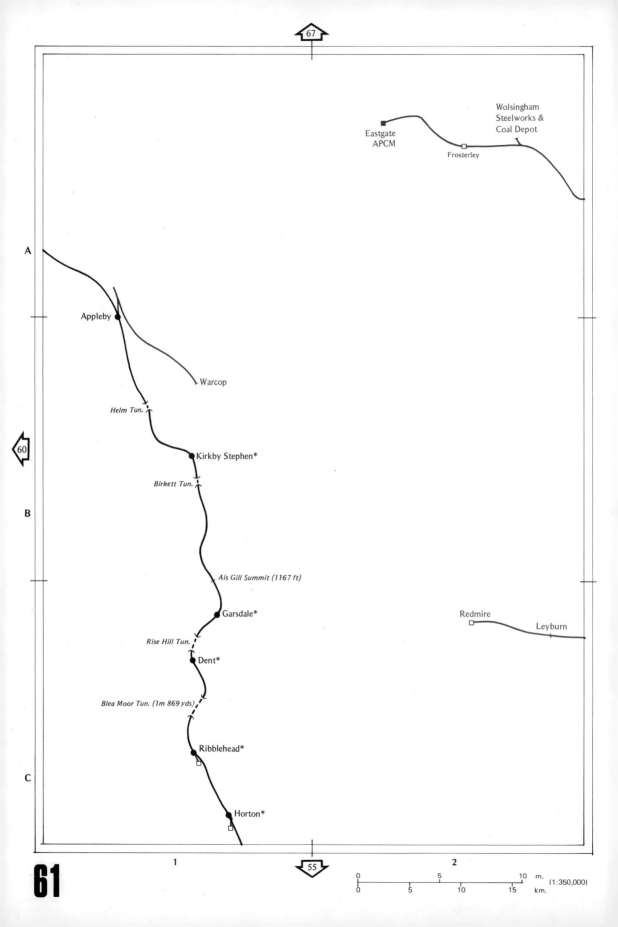

Wolsingham
Steelworks &
Coal Depot

Eastgate
APCM

Frosterley

A

Appleby

Warcop

Helm Tun.

Kirkby Stephen*

Birkett Tun.

B

Ais Gill Summit (1167 ft)

Garsdale*

Redmire

Leyburn

Rise Hill Tun.

Dent*

Blea Moor Tun. (1m 869 yds)

Ribblehead*

C

Horton*

1

2

| 0 | | 5 | | 10 | m. |
| 0 | 5 | | 10 | 15 | km. |

(1:350,000)

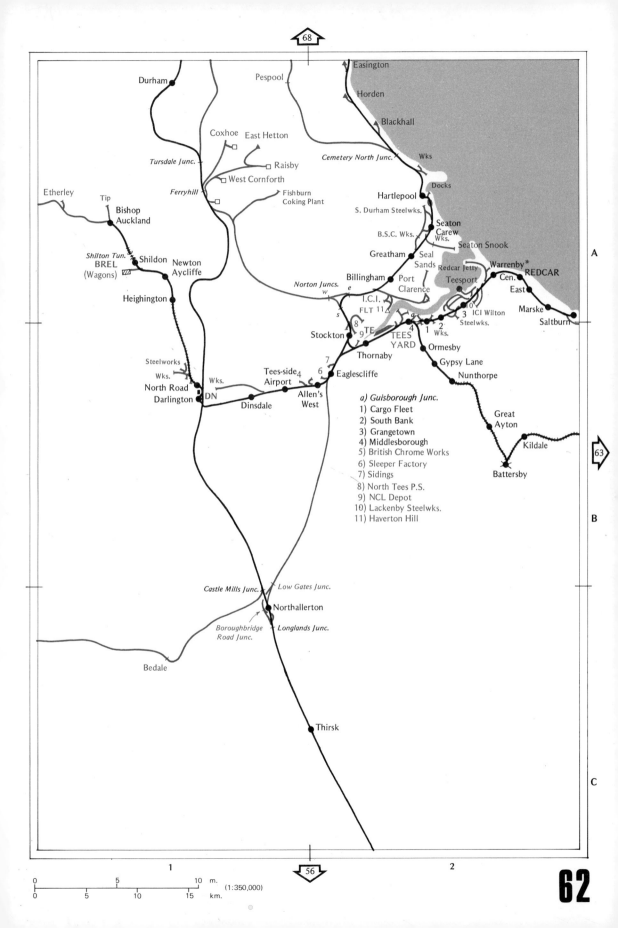

Durham

Pespool

Easington

Horden

Blackhall

Coxhoe   East Hetton

Tursdale Junc.   Raisby

West Cornforth

Ferryhill   Fishburn
Coking Plant

Cemetery North Junc.   Wks

Hartlepool

Docks

S. Durham Steelwks.

Seaton
Carew

B.S.C. Wks.   Wks.

Seaton Snook

Etherley   Tip

Bishop
Auckland

Greatham

Seal
Sands

Redcar Jetty

Warrenby*

Shilton Tun.
BREL
(Wagons)

Shildon

Newton
Aycliffe

Billingham   Port
Clarence

Teesport   Cen.   REDCAR
East

Heighington

Norton Juncs.
w
e

I.C.I.
FLT 11   ICI Wilton
Steelwks.

Marske

Saltburn

s

2
Wks.

Stockton

8

TE
9

TEES
YARD

g
4
1

10

ICI Wilton
Steelwks.

Thornaby

Ormesby

Gypsy Lane

Steelworks   7
6

Wks.   Wks.

Tees-side
Airport   4

Eaglescliffe

Nunthorpe

North Road
Darlington   DN

Dinsdale

Allen's
West

a) Guisborough Junc.
1) Cargo Fleet
2) South Bank
3) Grangetown
4) Middlesborough
5) British Chrome Works
6) Sleeper Factory
7) Sidings
8) North Tees P.S.
9) NCL Depot
10) Lackenby Steelwks.
11) Haverton Hill

Great
Ayton

Kildale

Battersby

A

B

63

Castle Mills Junc.   *Low Gates Junc.*

Northallerton

*Boroughbridge
Road Junc.*   *Longlands Junc.*

Bedale

Thirsk

C

0   5   10   m.
0   5   10   15   km.   (1:350,000)

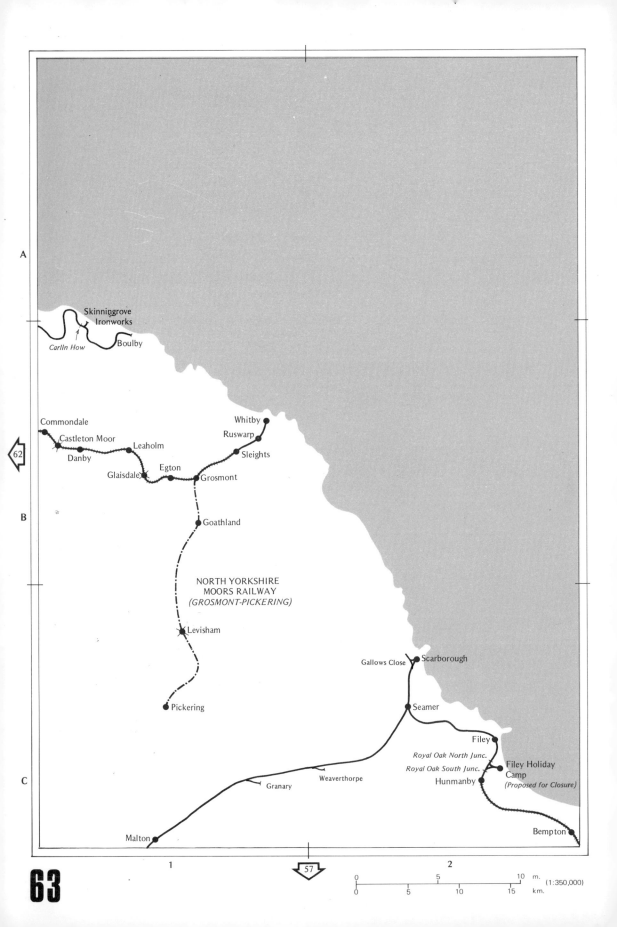

Skinningrove
Ironworks

Carlin How Boulby

Commondale Whitby
Castleton Moor Ruswarp
Danby Leaholm Sleights
Glaisdale Egton Grosmont

62

Goathland

B

NORTH YORKSHIRE
MOORS RAILWAY
(GROSMONT-PICKERING)

Levisham

Scarborough
Gallows Close

Pickering

Seamer

Filey

Royal Oak North Junc.
Royal Oak South Junc. Filey Holiday
Camp
Weaverthorpe Hunmanby *(Proposed for Closure)*

C Granary

Malton Bempton

63

1 2

57

0   5   10 m. (1:350,000)
0   5   10   15 km.

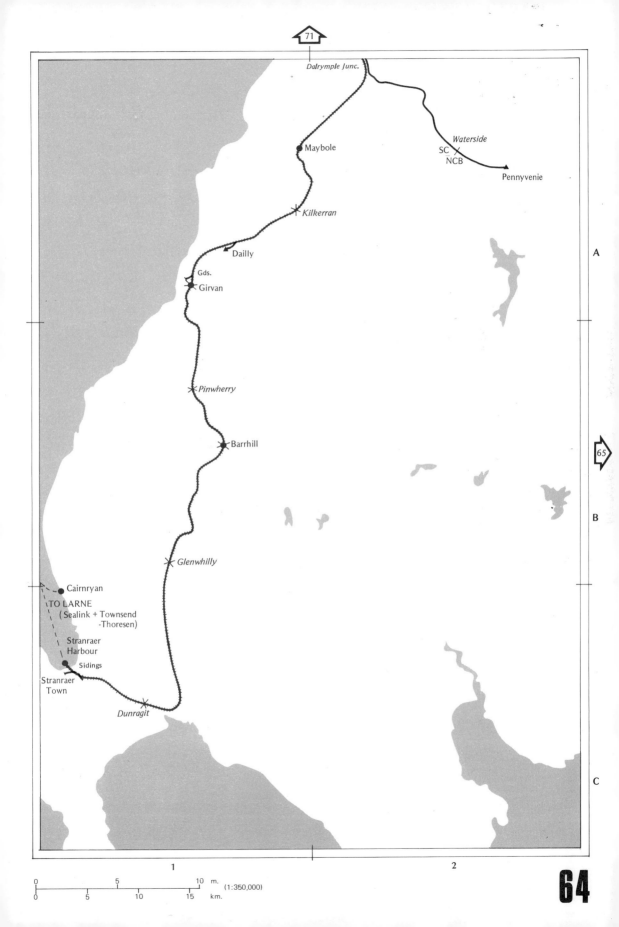

Dalrymple Junc.

Waterside
SC
NCB
Pennyvenie

Maybole

Kilkerran

Dailly

Gds.
Girvan

Pinwherry

Barrhill

65

Glenwhilly

Cairnryan
TO LARNE
(Sealink + Townsend
-Thoresen)

Stranraer
Harbour
Sidings

Stranraer
Town

Dunragit

A

B

C

1   2

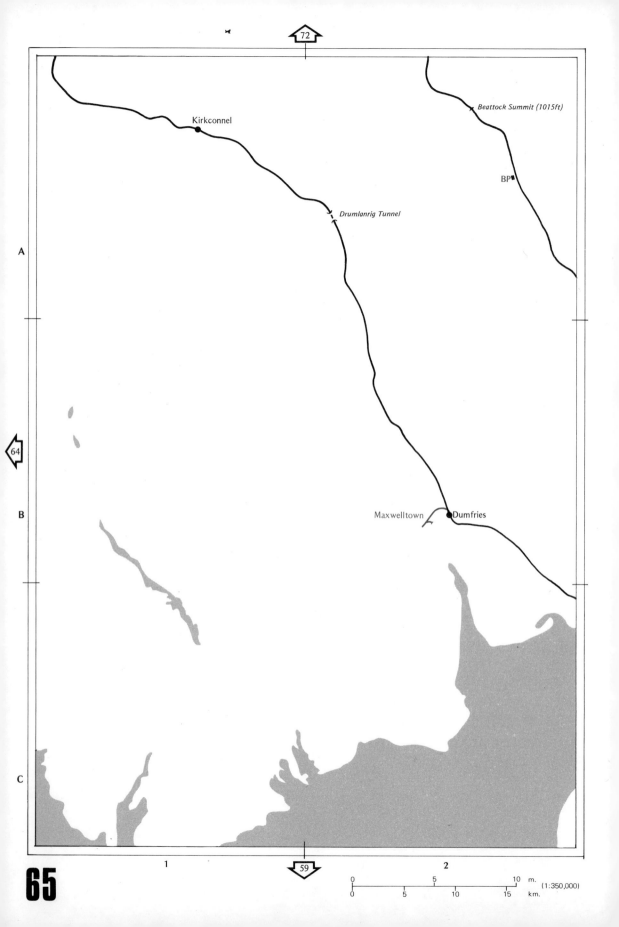

Kirkconnel

Beattock Summit (1015ft)

BP

Drumlanrig Tunnel

A

64

B

Maxwelltown Dumfries

C

1

2

65

```
0          5          10   m.   (1:350,000)
0     5      10      15   km.
```

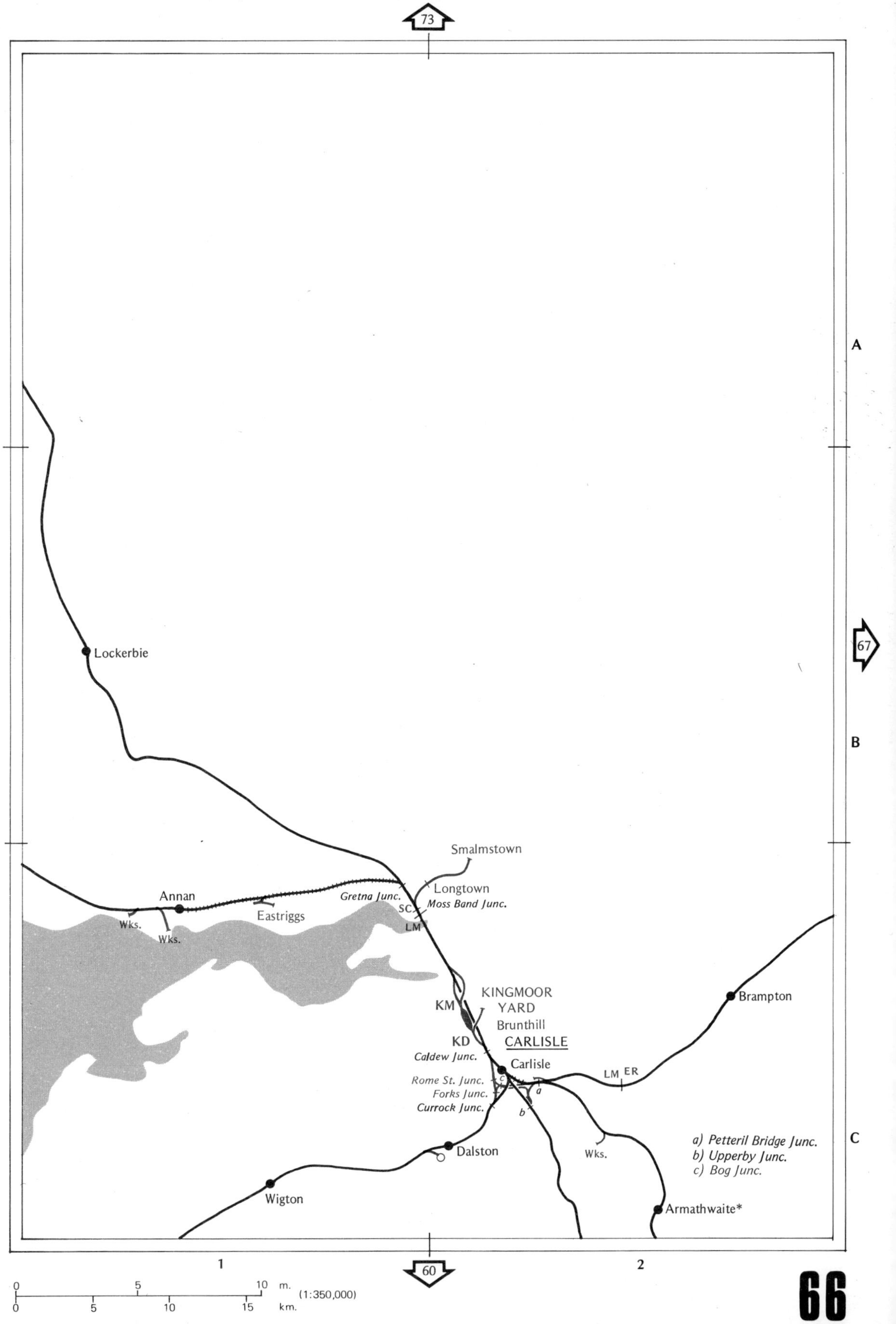

73

A

67

B

Lockerbie

Smalmstown

Annan
Eastriggs
Wks.
Wks.
Gretna Junc.
SC.
LM
Longtown
Moss Band Junc.

Brampton

KINGMOOR
YARD
KM
Brunthill
KD
CARLISLE
Caldew Junc.
Carlisle
Rome St. Junc.
Forks Junc.
Currock Junc.
c
a
b
LM ER

Wks.

a) Petteril Bridge Junc.
b) Upperby Junc.
c) Bog Junc.

C

Dalston

Wigton

Armathwaite*

1

60

2

0   5   10   m.   (1:350,000)
0   5   10   15   km.

66

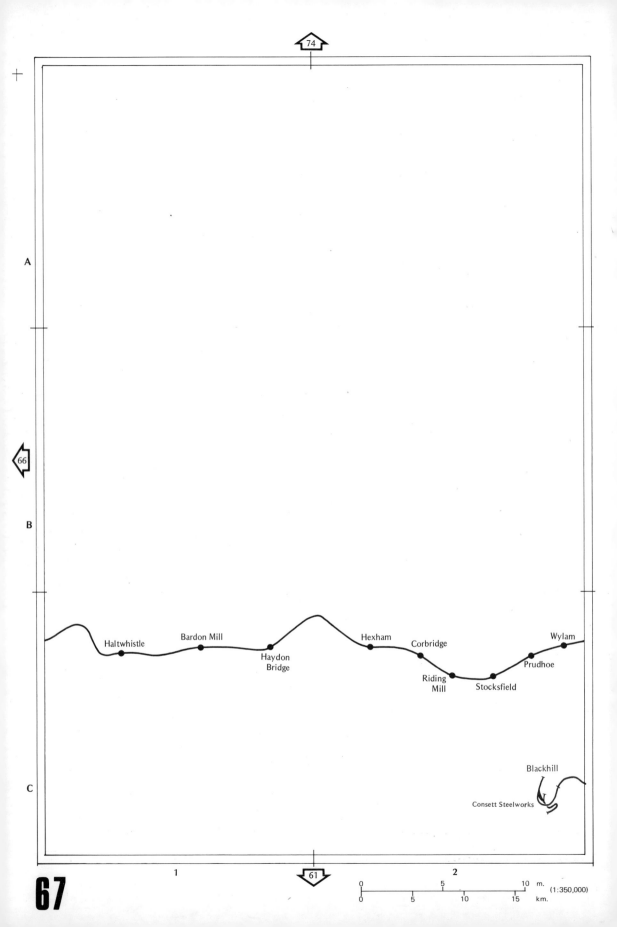

A

66

B

Haltwhistle

Bardon Mill

Haydon
Bridge

Hexham

Corbridge

Wylam

Prudhoe

Riding
Mill

Stocksfield

Blackhill

C

Consett Steelworks

1

2

67

0   5   10 m.   (1:350,000)

0   5   10   15   km.

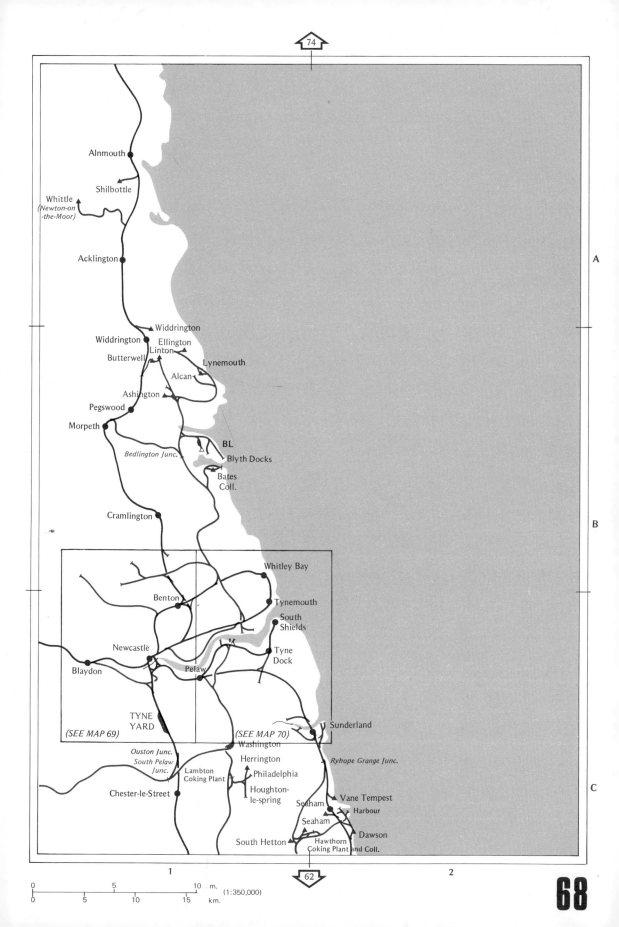

Alnmouth

Shilbottle

Whittle
*(Newton-on
-the-Moor)*

Acklington

Widdrington

Widdrington
Ellington
Linton
Butterwell
Lynemouth
Alcan
Ashington
Pegswood
Morpeth
Bedlington Junc.

BL
Blyth Docks
Bates
Coll.

Cramlington

Whitley Bay

Benton
Tynemouth
South
Shields

Newcastle
Tyne
Dock
Blaydon
Pelaw

TYNE
YARD
Sunderland

(SEE MAP 69)
(SEE MAP 70)
Washington

Ouston Junc.
*South Pelaw
Junc.*
Herrington
Ryhope Grange Junc.
Lambton
Coking Plant
Philadelphia
Houghton-
le-spring
Chester-le-Street
Vane Tempest
Seaham
Harbour
Seaham
Dawson
South Hetton
Hawthorn
Coking Plant and Coll.

A

B

C

1
2

0   5   10 m. (1:350,000)
0   5   10   15 km.

68

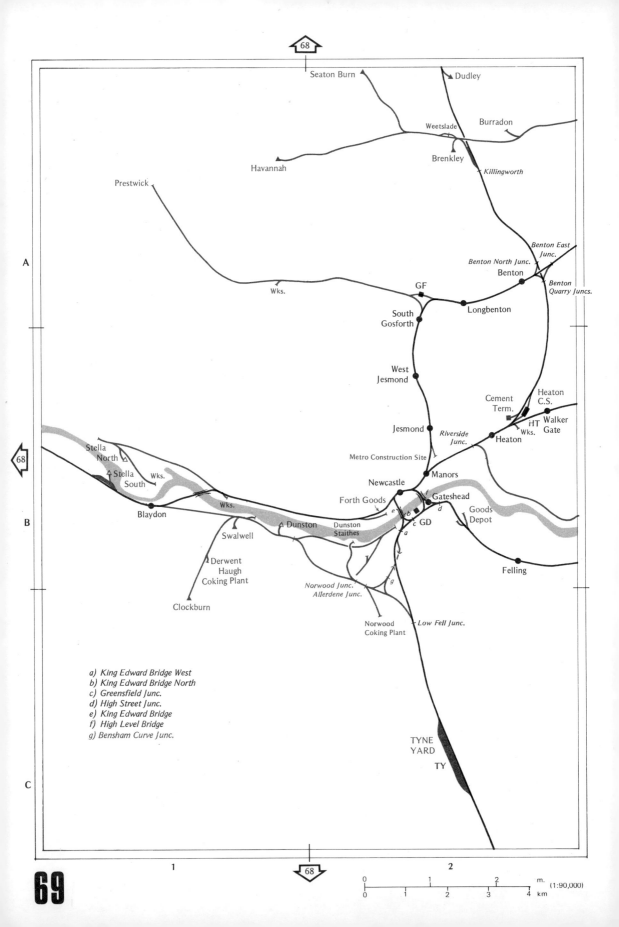

Seaton Burn

Dudley

Weetslade

Burradon

Havannah

Brenkley

Killingworth

Prestwick

Benton East
Junc.

Benton North Junc.

Benton

GF

Benton
Quarry Juncs.

South
Gosforth

Longbenton

West
Jesmond

Heaton
C.S.

Cement
Term.

HT

Walker
Gate

Jesmond

*Riverside
Junc.*

Wks.

Heaton

Metro Construction Site

Manors

Stella
North

Stella
South

Wks.

Newcastle

Forth Goods

Gateshead

Goods
Depot

f

Wks.

e

b

Blaydon

d

c GD

Swalwell

Dunston

Dunston
Staithes

a

Derwent
Haugh
Coking Plant

Felling

Norwood Junc.
Allerdene Junc.

g

Clockburn

Norwood
Coking Plant

Low Fell Junc.

a) King Edward Bridge West
b) King Edward Bridge North
c) Greensfield Junc.
d) High Street Junc.
e) King Edward Bridge
f) High Level Bridge
g) Bensham Curve Junc.

TYNE
YARD

TY

69

1

2

0   1   2
m.   (1:90,000)
0   1   2   3   4 km

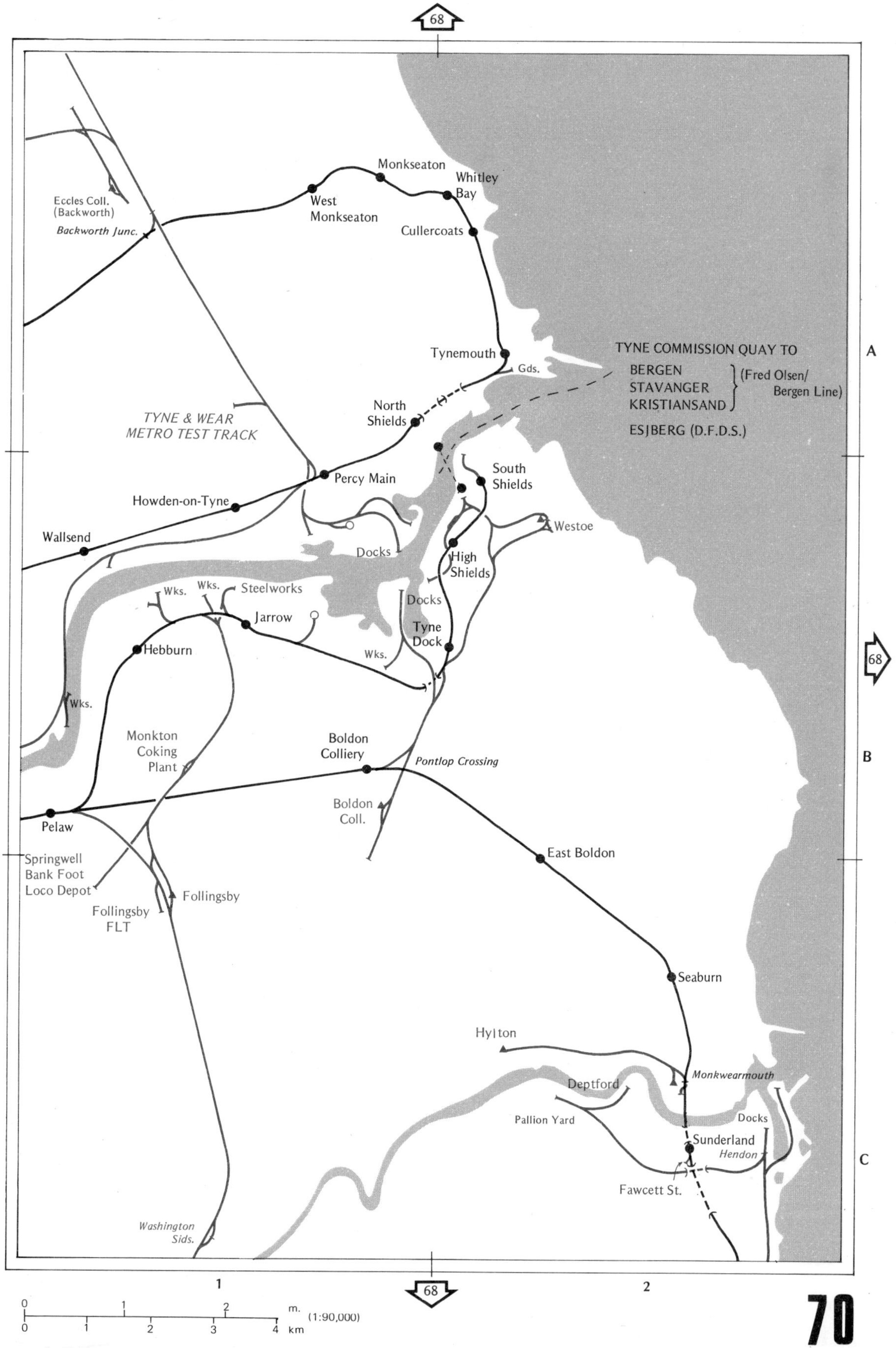

Eccles Coll.
(Backworth)
Backworth Junc.

Monkseaton

Whitley
Bay

West
Monkseaton

Cullercoats

*TYNE & WEAR
METRO TEST TRACK*

Tynemouth

Gds.

North
Shields

TYNE COMMISSION QUAY TO

BERGEN
STAVANGER   } (Fred Olsen/
KRISTIANSAND } Bergen Line)

ESJBERG (D.F.D.S.)

A

Percy Main

South
Shields

Howden-on-Tyne

Westoe

Wallsend

Docks

High
Shields

Wks.   Wks.   Steelworks

Docks

Jarrow

Tyne
Dock

Hebburn

Wks.

Wks.

Monkton
Coking
Plant

Boldon
Colliery

Pontlop Crossing

B

Pelaw

Boldon
Coll.

Springwell
Bank Foot
Loco Depot

East Boldon

Follingsby

Follingsby
FLT

68

Seaburn

Hylton

Monkwearmouth

Deptford

Docks

Pallion Yard

Sunderland
Hendon

C

Fawcett St.

*Washington
Sids.*

1

m. (1:90,000)

0   1   2   3   4 km

2

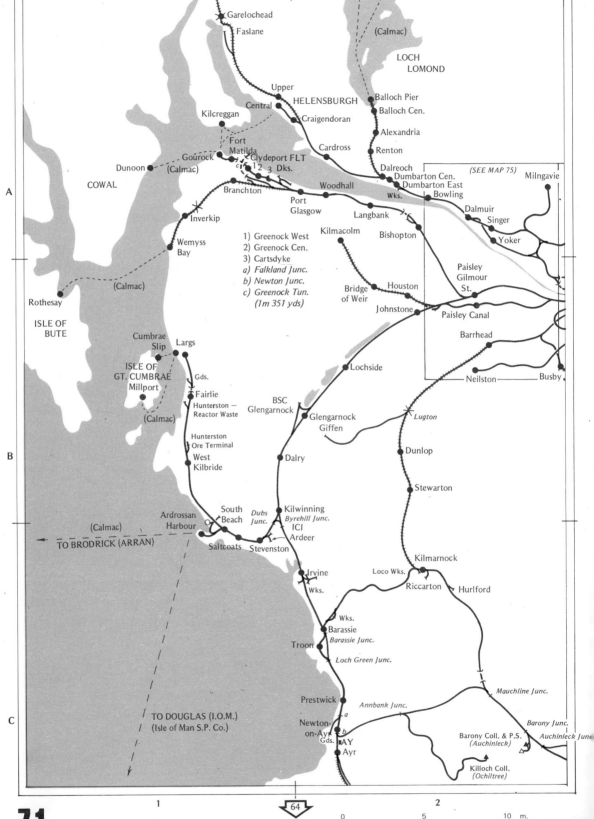

Garelochead
Faslane

(Calmac)

LOCH
LOMOND

Upper
Central
HELENSBURGH
Craigendoran

Kilcreggan

Balloch Pier
Balloch Cen.

Alexandria

Cardross

Renton

Fort
Matilda
Gourock
(Calmac)
Clydeport FLT
1 2 3 Dks.

Dunoon

Dalreoch
Dumbarton Cen.
Dumbarton East
Bowling

(SEE MAP 75)

Milngavie

COWAL

Branchton

Woodhall
Wks.

Dalmuir
Singer

Port
Glasgow

Langbank

Yoker

Inverkip

1) Greenock West
2) Greenock Cen.
3) Cartsdyke
a) Falkland Junc.
b) Newton Junc.
c) Greenock Tun.
  (1m 351 yds)

Kilmacolm

Bishopton

Paisley
Gilmour
St.

Wemyss
Bay

Rothesay

(Calmac)

Bridge
of Weir

Houston

Johnstone

Paisley Canal

Barrhead

ISLE OF
BUTE

Cumbrae
Slip
Largs

ISLE OF
GT. CUMBRAE
Millport

Gds.

Fairlie

Lochside

Neilston

Busby

Hunterston —
Reactor Waste

BSC
Glengarnock

Glengarnock
Giffen

Lugton

Dunlop

Hunterston
Ore Terminal
West
Kilbride

Dalry

Stewarton

Ardrossan
Harbour

South
Beach

Dubs
Junc.

Kilwinning
Byrehill Junc.
ICI
Ardeer

Kilmarnock

(Calmac)

TO BRODRICK (ARRAN)

Saltcoats

Stevenston

Loco Wks.

Riccarton

Hurlford

Irvine
Wks.

Wks.
Barassie
Barassie Junc.

Troon

Loch Green Junc.

Mauchline Junc.

TO DOUGLAS (I.O.M.)
(Isle of Man S.P. Co.)

Prestwick

Annbank Junc.

Barony Junc.

Newton-
on-Ayr
Gds.

a

b

AY

Barony Coll. & P.S.
(Auchinleck)

Auchinleck Junc.

Ayr

Killoch Coll.
(Ochiltree)

1

2

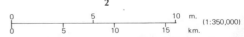

0   5   10 m.
(1:350,000)
0   5   10   15 km.

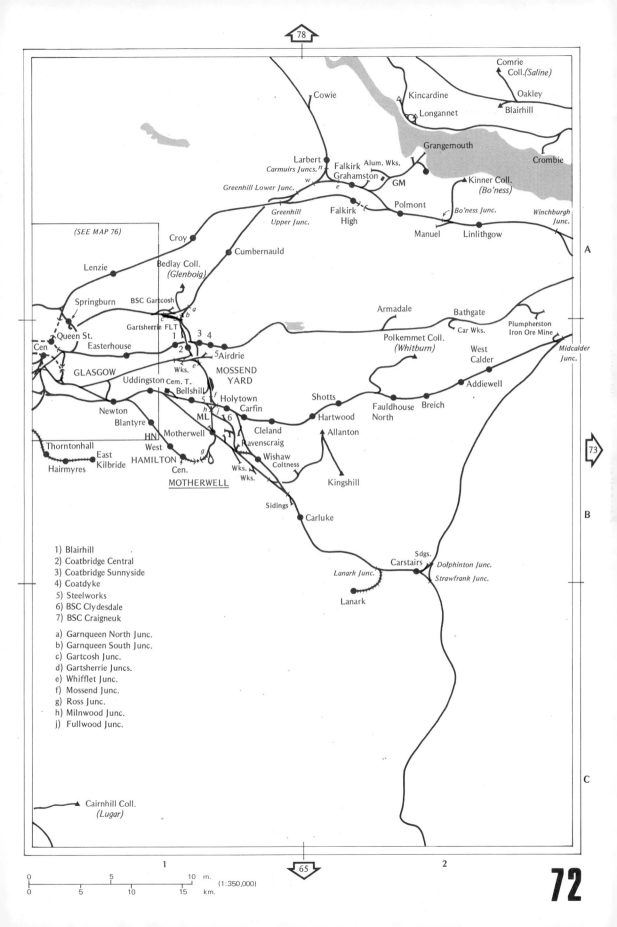

Comrie
Coll.*(Saline)*
Oakley
Blairhill
Kincardine
Longannet
Grangemouth
Crombie
Cowie
Larbert
Carmuirs Juncs. n
Falkirk
Grahamston
Alum. Wks.
Greenhill Lower Junc.
w
e
GM
Kinner Coll.
(Bo'ness)
Greenhill
Upper Junc.
Falkirk
High
Polmont
Bo'ness Junc.
*Winchburgh
Junc.*
Croy
Cumbernauld
Manuel
Linlithgow
A
(SEE MAP 76)
Bedlay Coll.
(Glenboig)
Lenzie
Springburn
BSC Gartcosh
Armadale
Bathgate
Car Wks.
Plumpherston
Iron Ore Mine
Gartsherrie FLT
a
c
b
Polkemmet Coll.
(Whitburn)
West
Calder
*Midcalder
Junc.*
Queen St.
Cen
Easterhouse
1
3 4
2
5 Airdrie
Wks.
e
MOSSEND
YARD
Addiewell
GLASGOW
Uddingston Cem. T.
Bellshill
f
Holytown
Carfin
Shotts
Fauldhouse
North
Breich
Newton
Blantyre
5
h
j
ML
6
Cleland
Hartwood
Allanton
HN
West
Motherwell
T
7
Ravenscraig
Wishaw
Coltness
Thorntonhall
East
Kilbride
HAMILTON
g
Cen.
Wks.
Wks.
Kingshill
Hairmyres
MOTHERWELL
Sidings
Carluke
B
Sdgs.
Carstairs
Dolphinton Junc.
Lanark Junc.
Strawfrank Junc.
Lanark
C

1) Blairhill
2) Coatbridge Central
3) Coatbridge Sunnyside
4) Coatdyke
5) Steelworks
6) BSC Clydesdale
7) BSC Craigneuk

a) Garnqueen North Junc.
b) Garnqueen South Junc.
c) Gartcosh Junc.
d) Gartsherrie Juncs.
e) Whifflet Junc.
f) Mossend Junc.
g) Ross Junc.
h) Milnwood Junc.
j) Fullwood Junc.

Cairnhill Coll.
(Lugar)

73

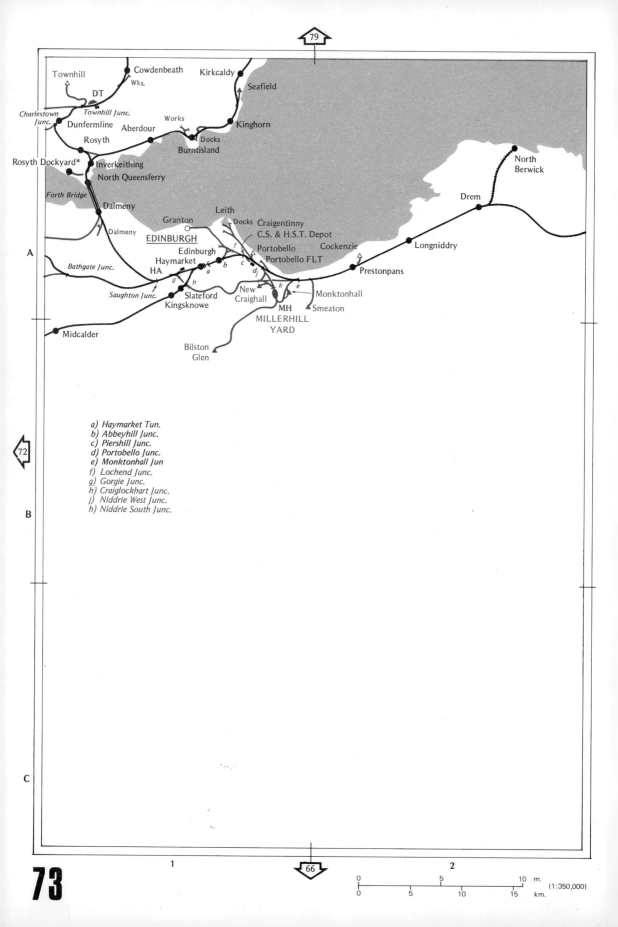

Townhill

Cowdenbeath

Kirkcaldy

Wks.

Seafield

DT

Charlestown Junc.

Townhill Junc.

Dunfermline

Aberdour

Works

Kinghorn

Rosyth

Docks

Burntisland

Rosyth Dockyard*

Inverkeithing

North Queensferry

North Berwick

Forth Bridge

Dalmeny

Drem

Granton

Leith

Dalmeny

Docks

Craigentinny
C.S. & H.S.T. Depot

Cockenzie

Longniddry

EDINBURGH

Edinburgh

Portobello

Bathgate Junc.

Haymarket

f

Portobello FLT

HA

a

b

c

d

Prestonpans

g

h

Monktonhall

Saughton Junc.

Slateford

New
Craighall

k

e

Kingsknowe

MH

Smeaton

Midcalder

MILLERHILL
YARD

Bilston
Glen

A

B

72

C

a) Haymarket Tun.
b) Abbeyhill Junc.
c) Piershill Junc.
d) Portobello Junc.
e) Monktonhall Jun
f) Lochend Junc.
g) Gorgie Junc.
h) Craiglockhart Junc.
j) Niddrie West Junc.
h) Niddrie South Junc.

0   5   10 m.

0   5   10   15 km.

(1:350,000)

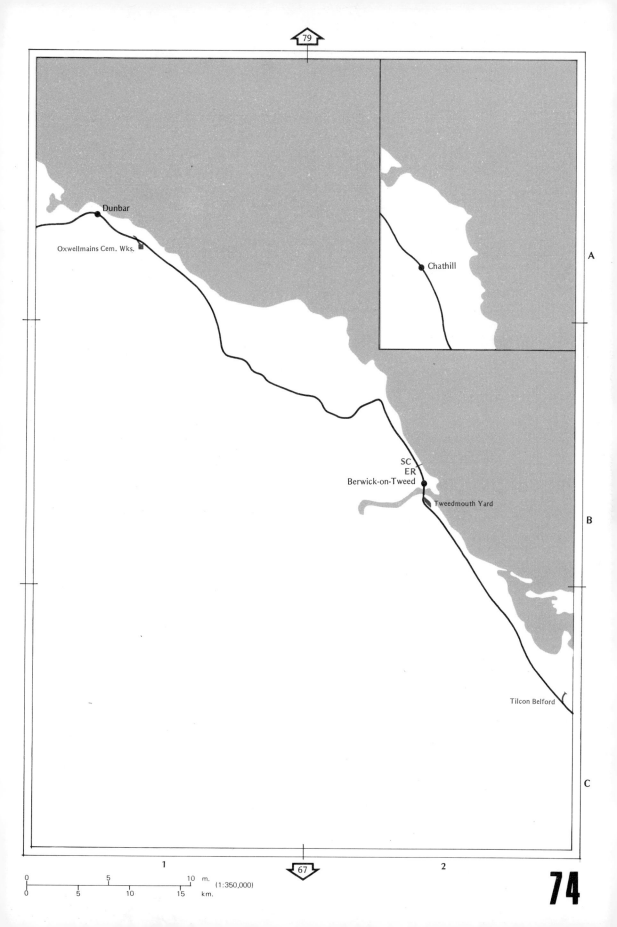

79

Dunbar

Oxwellmains Cem. Wks.

Chathill

A

SC
ER
Berwick-on-Tweed

Tweedmouth Yard

B

Tilcon Belford

C

1

67

2

0   5   10 m.   (1:350,000)

0   5   10   15   km.

74

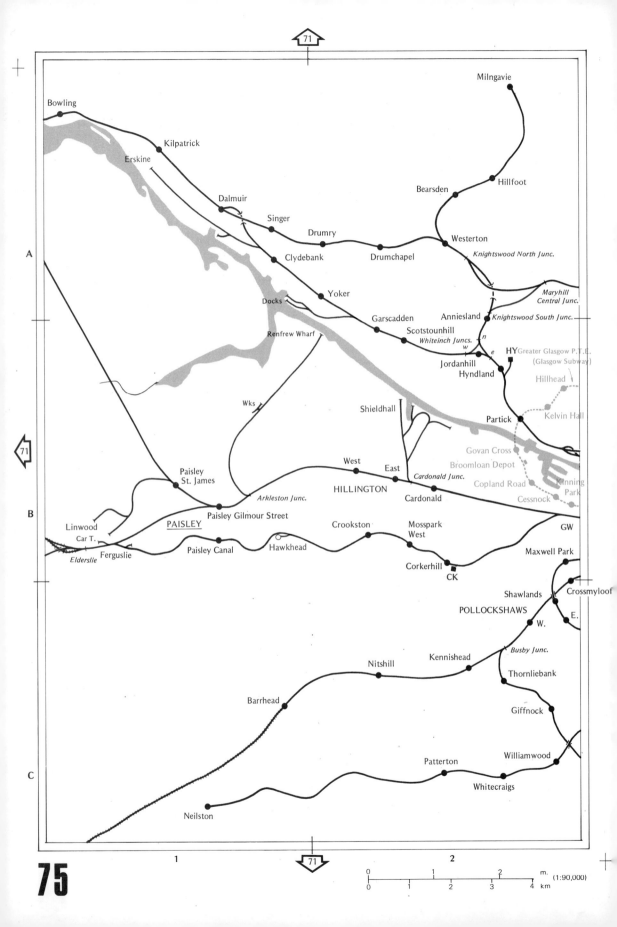

Milngavie

Bowling

Kilpatrick

Erskine

Dalmuir

Singer

Drumry

Clydebank

Drumchapel

Bearsden

Hillfoot

Westerton

Knightswood North Junc.

Yoker

Docks

Garscadden

Scotstounhill

Anniesland

Knightswood South Junc.

Maryhill Central Junc.

Renfrew Wharf

Whiteinch Juncs.

n

w

e

Jordanhill

Hyndland

HY Greater Glasgow P.T.E.
(Glasgow Subway)

Hillhead

Wks

Shieldhall

Partick

Kelvin Hall

Govan Cross

Broomloan Depot

West

East

Cardonald Junc.

HILLINGTON

Copland Road

Kinning Park

Paisley
St. James

Cardonald

Cessnock

Arkleston Junc.

PAISLEY

Paisley Gilmour Street

Crookston

Mosspark
West

GW

Linwood
Car T.

Ferguslie

Paisley Canal

Hawkhead

Corkerhill

CK

Maxwell Park

Elderslie

Crossmyloof

Shawlands

E.

POLLOCKSHAWS

W.

Busby Junc.

Kennishead

Thornliebank

Nitshill

Giffnock

Barrhead

Williamwood

Patterton

Whitecraigs

Neilston

1

2

m. (1:90,000)

0   1   2

0 1 2 3 4 km

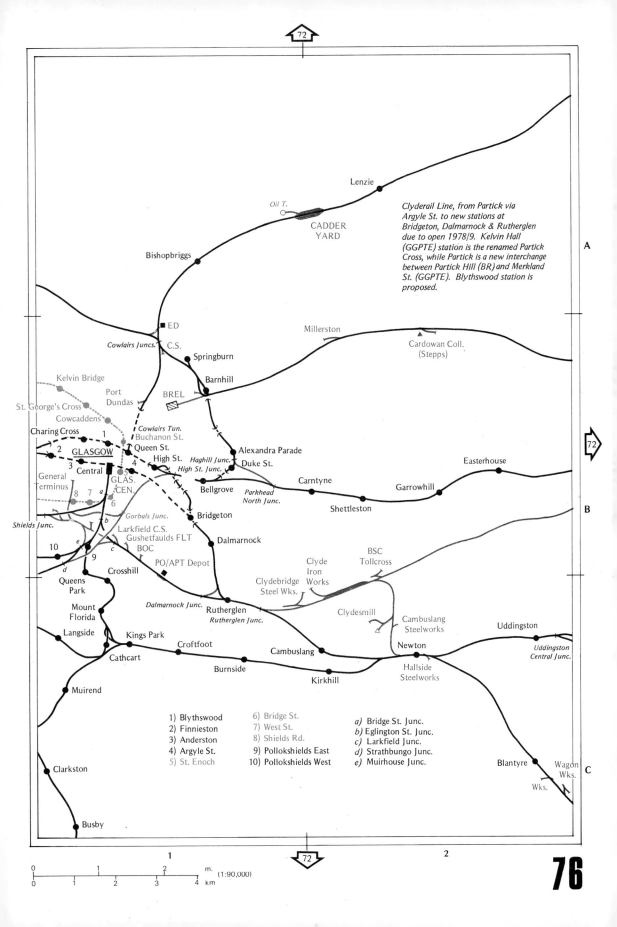

Lenzie

Oil T.

CADDER YARD

Clyderail Line, from Partick via Argyle St. to new stations at Bridgeton, Dalmarnock & Rutherglen due to open 1978/9. Kelvin Hall (GGPTE) station is the renamed Partick Cross, while Partick is a new interchange between Partick Hill (BR) and Merkland St. (GGPTE). Blythswood station is proposed.

Bishopbriggs

A

ED

Cowlairs Juncs.   C.S.

Springburn

Barnhill

Millerston

Cardowan Coll. (Stepps)

Kelvin Bridge

Port Dundas

BREL

St. George's Cross

Cowcaddens

Charing Cross   1

Cowlairs Tun.
Buchanon St.

2   GLASGOW   Queen St.

3   Central   4   High St.   *Haghill Junc.*
Duke St.

GLAS. CEN.   *High St. Junc.*

Alexandra Parade

Easterhouse

General Terminus   8   7   a   6

Bellgrove   *Parkhead North Junc.*

Carntyne

Garrowhill

Shields Junc.   b   *Gorbals Junc.*

Bridgeton

Shettleston

B

10   e   Larkfield C.S.
Gushetfaulds FLT

9   c   BOC

Dalmarnock

Clyde Iron Works

BSC Tollcross

Crosshill   PO/APT Depot

d

Queens Park

Clydebridge Steel Wks.

Clydesmill

Cambuslang Steelworks

Uddingston

Mount Florida

Langside   Kings Park

Croftfoot

Dalmarnock Junc.

Rutherglen
Rutherglen Junc.

Cambuslang

Newton

Uddingston Central Junc.

Cathcart

Burnside

Kirkhill

Hallside Steelworks

Muirend

Clarkston

1) Blythswood	6) Bridge St.	a) Bridge St. Junc.	
2) Finnieston	7) West St.	b) Eglington St. Junc.	
3) Anderston	8) Shields Rd.	c) Larkfield Junc.	
4) Argyle St.	9) Pollokshields East	d) Strathbungo Junc.	
5) St. Enoch	10) Pollokshields West	e) Muirhouse Junc.	

Blantyre   Wagon Wks.

Wks.

C

Busby

0   1   2
m. (1:90,000)
0   1   2   3   4   km

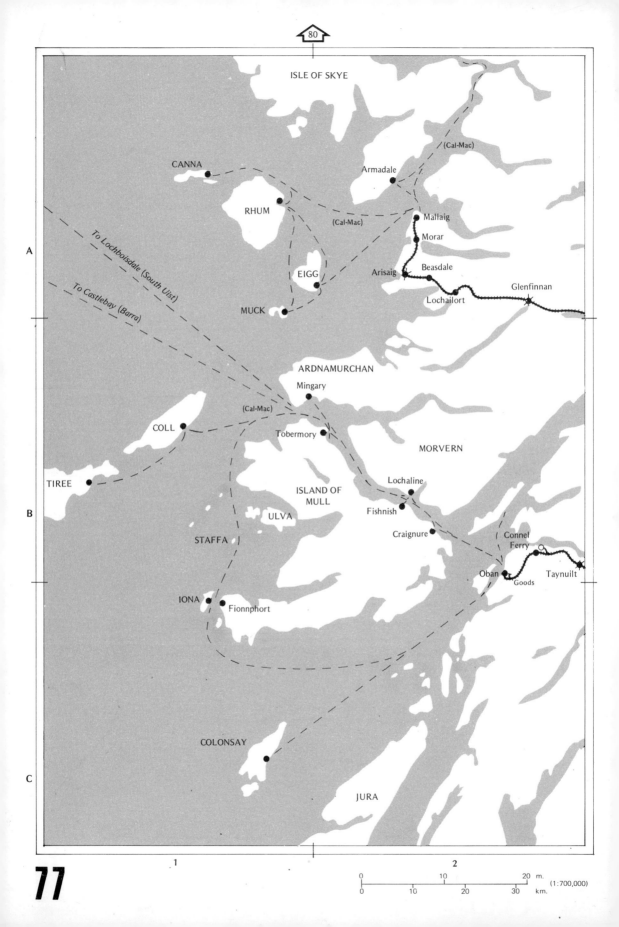

ISLE OF SKYE

CANNA

RHUM

To Lochboisdale (South Uist)

To Castlebay (Barra)

A

EIGG

MUCK

Armadale

(Cal-Mac)

(Cal-Mac)

Mallaig

Morar

Beasdale

Arisaig

Lochailort

Glenfinnan

ARDNAMURCHAN

Mingary

(Cal-Mac)

COLL

Tobermory

MORVERN

Lochaline

TIREE

ISLAND OF
MULL

Fishnish

B

ULVA

STAFFA

Craignure

Connel
Ferry

Oban

Taynuilt

Goods

IONA

Fionnphort

COLONSAY

C

JURA

1

2

0   10   20 m.

0   10   20   30 km.

(1:700,000)

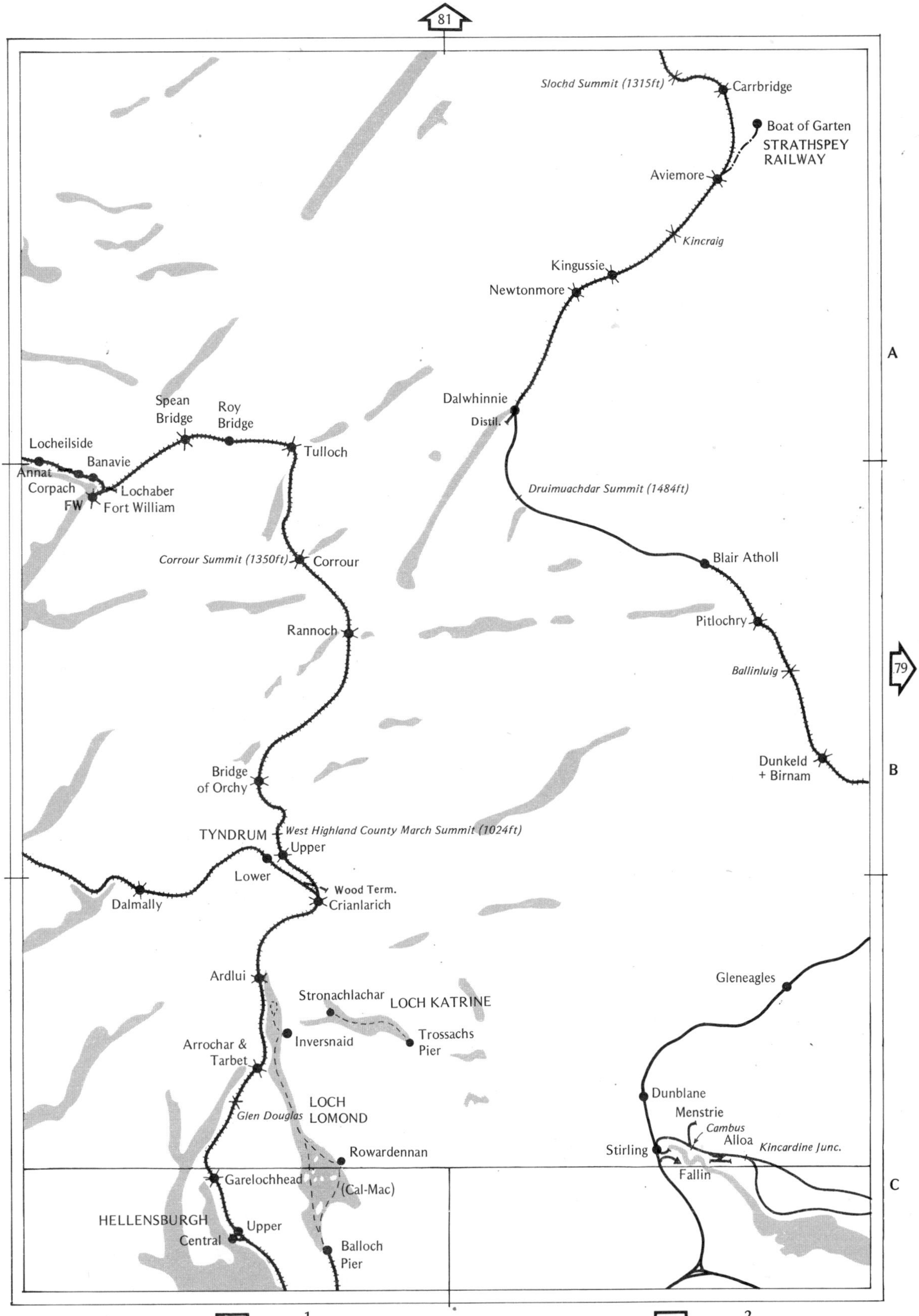

Slochd Summit (1315ft) Carrbridge

Boat of Garten
STRATHSPEY RAILWAY

Aviemore

Kincraig

Kingussie

Newtonmore

A

Dalwhinnie
Distil.

Druimuachdar Summit (1484ft)

Blair Atholl

Pitlochry

Ballinluig

Dunkeld + Birnam

B

Spean Bridge   Roy Bridge

Locheilside
Banavie   Tulloch
Annat
Corpach   Lochaber
FW   Fort William

Corrour Summit (1350ft)   Corrour

Rannoch

Bridge of Orchy

TYNDRUM   *West Highland County March Summit (1024ft)*
Upper
Lower
Wood Term.
Crianlarich

Dalmally

Ardlui
Stronachlachar   **LOCH KATRINE**
Inversnaid   Trossachs Pier

Gleneagles

Arrochar & Tarbet
Glen Douglas   **LOCH LOMOND**

Dunblane
Menstrie
Cambus   Alloa   *Kincardine Junc.*
Stirling
Fallin

Rowardennan

Garelochhead   (Cal-Mac)

C

HELLENSBURGH
Central   Upper

Balloch Pier

1   2

0   10   20 m.
0   10   20   30 km.   (1:700,000)

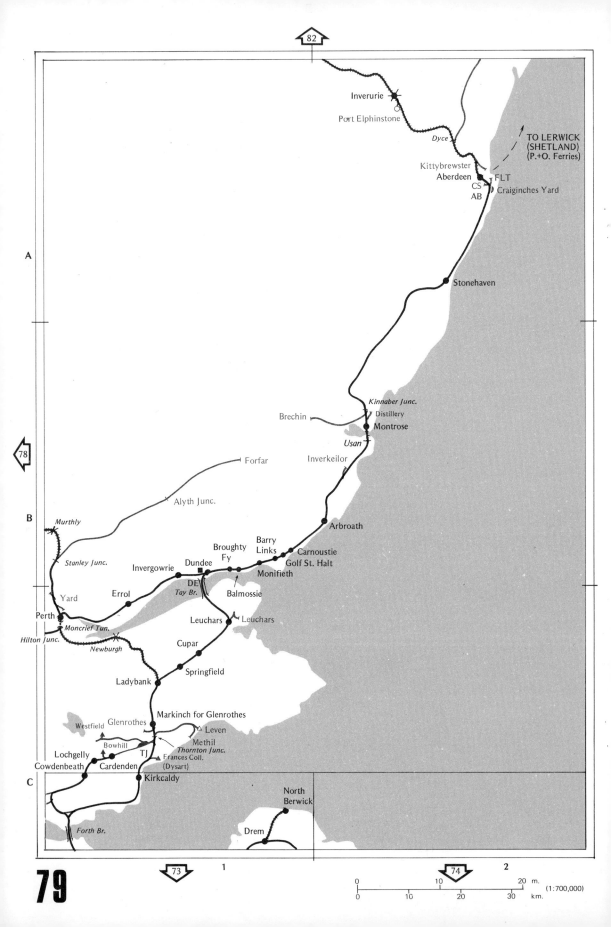

Inverurie

Port Elphinstone

Dyce

Kittybrewster

Aberdeen   FLT
        CS   Craiginches Yard
        AB

TO LERWICK
(SHETLAND)
(P.+O. Ferries)

Stonehaven

Kinnaber Junc.

Brechin   Distillery
        Montrose

Usan

Inverkeilor

Forfar

Alyth Junc.

Murthly

Arbroath

Stanley Junc.

Barry
Links
Broughty   Carnoustie
Fy   Golf St. Halt
Invergowrie   Dundee   Monifieth
Errol   DE
    Tay Br.   Balmossie

Yard

Perth
Moncrief Tun.
Hilton Junc.
    Newburgh

Leuchars   Leuchars

Cupar

Springfield

Ladybank

Markinch for Glenrothes

Westfield   Glenrothes   Leven
        Methil
Bowhill   Thornton Junc.
Lochgelly   TJ   Frances Coll.
Cowdenbeath   Cardenden   (Dysart)

Kirkcaldy

North
Berwick

Forth Br.   Drem

78

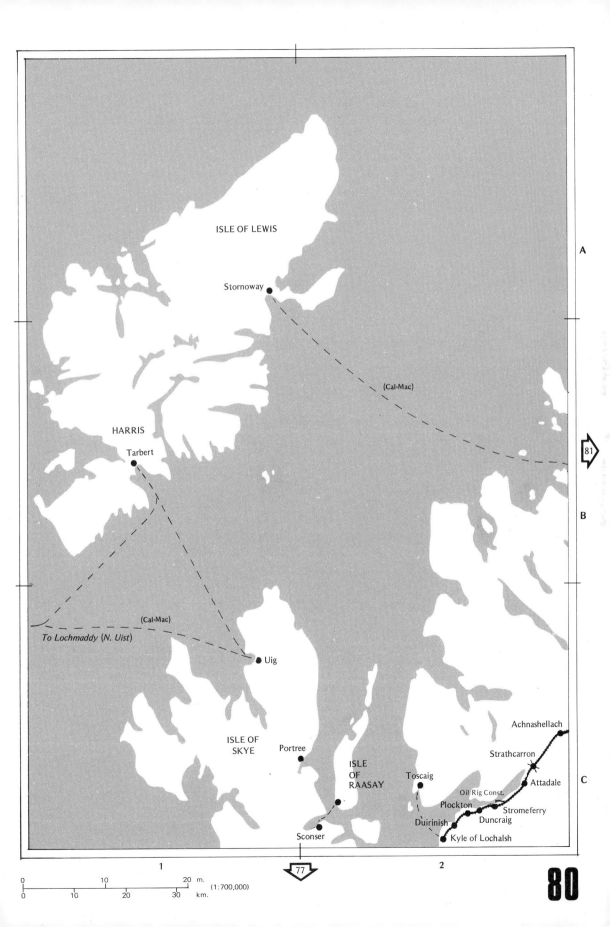

ISLE OF LEWIS

Stornoway

(Cal-Mac)

HARRIS

Tarbert

A

81

B

(Cal-Mac)

To Lochmaddy (N. Uist)

Uig

Achnashellach

ISLE OF
SKYE

Portree

Strathcarron

ISLE
OF
RAASAY

Toscaig

Attadale

C

Oil Rig Const.

Plockton

Duncraig

Stromeferry

Duirinish

Sconser

Kyle of Lochalsh

1

77

2

0   10   20 m.
0   10   20   30   (1:700,000)
                        km.

80

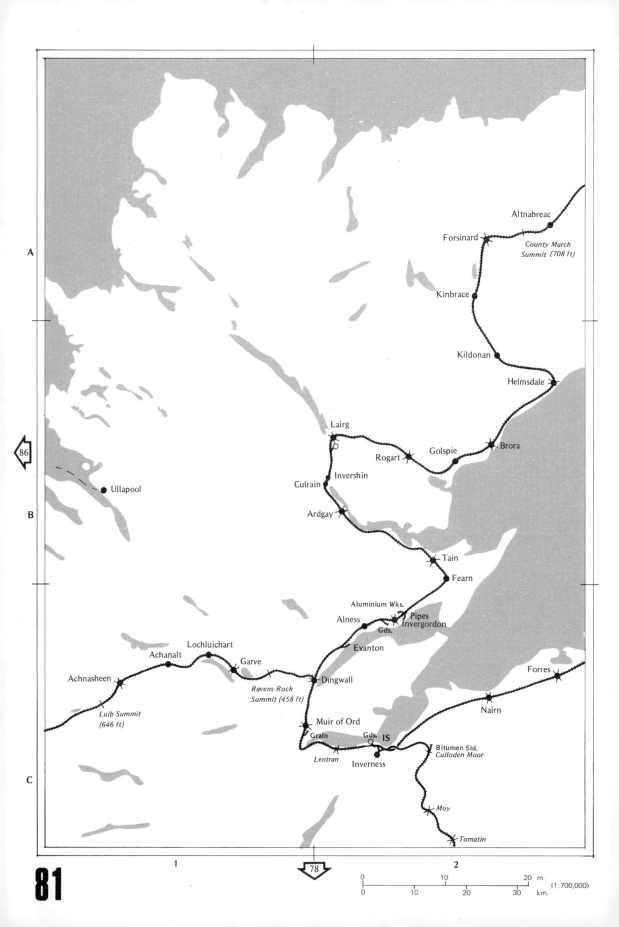

A

86

B

C

Altnabreac

Forsinard

County March Summit (708 ft)

Kinbrace

Kildonan

Helmsdale

Lairg

Rogart   Golspie   Brora

Invershin

Culrain

Ullapool

Ardgay

Tain

Fearn

Aluminium Wks.

Alness   Pipes
Invergordon
Gds.
Evanton

Lochluichart

Achanalt   Garve

Achnasheen   Dingwall

Ravens Rock Summit (458 ft)

Forres

Nairn

Luib Summit (646 ft)

Muir of Ord

Grain   Gds.   IS   Bitumen Sid.
Lentran   *Culloden Moor*
Inverness

Moy

Tomatin

81

78

0   10   20 m.
0   10   20   30 km.   (1:700,000)

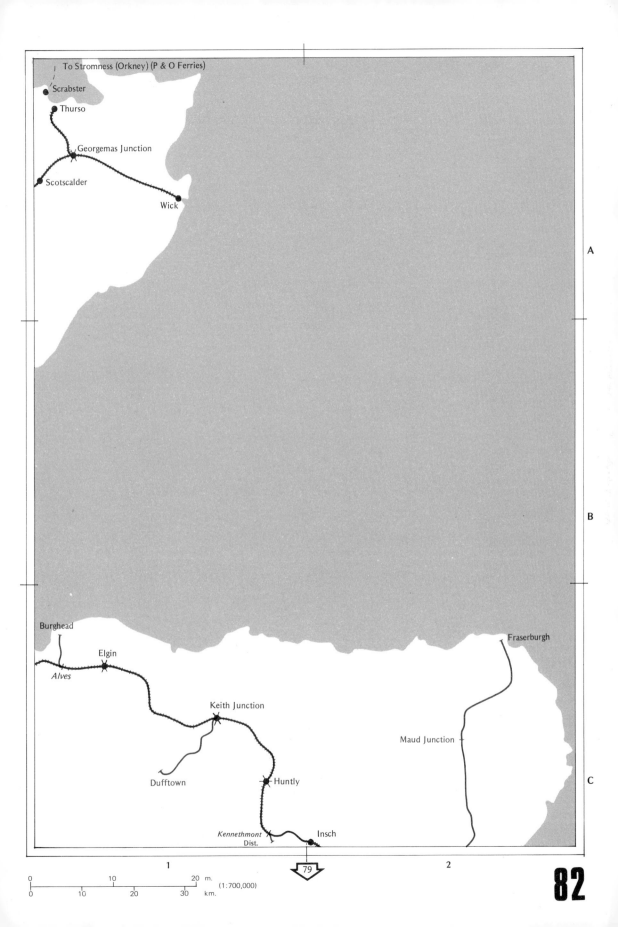

To Stromness (Orkney) (P & O Ferries)

Scrabster

Thurso

Georgemas Junction

Scotscalder

Wick

A

B

Burghead

Fraserburgh

Elgin

Alves

Keith Junction

Maud Junction

Dufftown

Huntly

C

Kennethmont
Dist.

Insch

1

79

2

0   10   20 m.
0   10   20   30   km.
(1:700,000)

82

INDEX TO PASSENGER STATIONS

For list of abbreviations see end of Passenger Station Index
(* Indicates unadvertised or excursion station)

Station	Region	No	Grid		Station	Region	No	Grid
Bamber Bridge	LM	54	B2		Belmont	SO	17	C1
Bamford	LM	47	A1		Belper	LM	47	C1
Banavie	SC	78	B1		Belsize Park	LT	21	A1
Banbury	LM	30	A2		Beltring & Branbridges	SO	12	A2
Bangor	LM	43	A2		Belvedere	SO	32	C2
Bank	SO/LT	21	B2		Bempton	ER	63	C2
Bank Hall	LM	53	B1		Benfleet	ER	33	C1
Banstead	SO	17	C1		Ben Rhydding	ER	55	A2
Barassie	SC	71	C2		Bentham	LM	55	A1
Barbican	LM/LT	21	B2		Bentley	SO	11	B1
Bardon Mill	ER	67	C1		Benton	ER	69	A2
Bare Lane	LM	54	A2		Bere Alston	WR	2	B2
Bargoed	WR	28	B1		Bere Ferrers	WR	2	B2
Barking	ER/LT	22	B2		Berkhamsted	LM	31	B2
Barkingside	LT	22	A2		Berkswell	LM	38	B1
Barlaston	LM	46	C1		Berney Arms	ER	42	A1
Barming	SO	13	A1		Berrylands	SO	16	B2
Barmouth	LM	34	A2		Berwick (Sussex)	SO	12	C2
Barmouth Ferry	FB	34	A2		Berwick-upon-Tweed	ER	74	B2
Barnehurst	SO	32	C2		Bescar Lane	LM	54	C2
Barnes	SO	20	C2		Bescot	LM	37	B2
Barnes Bridge	SO	20	C2		Besses o' th' Barn	LM	51	A2
Barnetby	ER	57	C2		Betchworth	SO	11	A2
Barnham	SO	11	C2		Bethnal Green	ER/LT	22	B1
Barnhill	SC	76	B1		Betws-y-Coed	LM	44	B1
Barnsley	ER	56	C1		Beverley	ER	57	B2
Barnstaple	WR	6	B2		Bewdley	SV	37	B1
Barnt Green	LM	37	B2		Bexhill	SO	13	C1
Barons Court	LT	21	C1		Bexley	SO	32	C2
Barrhead	SC	75	C1		Bexleyheath	SO	32	C2
Barrhill	SC	64	B1		Bicester	LM	30	A2
Barrow-in-Furness	LM	54	A1		Bickley	SO	18	B2
Barrow Haven	ER	57	B2		Bidston	LM	45	A1
Barry	WR	7	A2		Biggleswade	ER	31	A2
Barry Docks	WR	8	A1		Bilbrook	LM	37	A1
Barry Island	WR	7	A2		Billericay	ER	32	C2
Barry Links	SC	79	B1		Billingham	ER	62	A2
Barton-on-Humber	ER	57	B2		Billingshurst	SO	11	B2
Basildon	ER	32	C2		Bingham	LM	48	C1
Basingstoke	SO	10	A2		Bingham Road	SO	17	B2
Bat & Ball	SO	12	A2		Bingley	ER	55	B2
Bath Spa	WR	9	A1		Birchgrove	WR	28	C1
Batley	ER	56	B1		Birchington-on-Sea	SO	14	A1
Battersby	ER	62	B2		Birkbeck	SO	18	B1
Battersea Park	SO	21	C1		Birkdale	LM	54	C1
Battle	SO	13	C1		Birkenhead Central	LM	53	C1
Battlesbridge	ER	33	C1		Birkenhead Hamilton Square	LM	53	B1
Bayford	ER	32	B1		Birkenhead North	LM	53	B1
Bayswater	LT	21	B1		Birkenhead Park	LM	53	B1
Beaconsfield	LM	31	C1		Birmingham International	LM	38	B1
Bearley	LM	38	C1		Birmingham Moor Street	LM	38	B2
Bearsden	SC	75	A2		Birmingham New Street	LM	38	B2
Bearstead & Thurnham	SO	13	A1		Bishop Auckland	ER	62	A1
Beasdale	SC	77	A2		Bishopbriggs	SC	76	A1
Beaulieu Road	SO	10	C1		Bishops Stortford	ER	32	B2
Bebington & New Ferry	LM	53	C1		Bishopstone	SO	12	C2
Beccles	ER	42	B1		Bishopton	SC	71	A2
Beckenham Hill	SO	18	A1		Bispham	BF	54	B1
Beckenham Junction	SO	18	A1		Blackburn	LM	55	B1
Beckfoot	RE	60	B1		Blackfriars	SO/LT	21	B2
Becontree	LT	32	C1		Blackheath	SO	22	C1
Beddington Lane	SO	17	B2		Blackhorse Road	ER/LT	22	A1
Bedford Midland Road	LM	39	C2		Blackpool North	LM	54	B1
Bedford St. John's	LM	39	C2		Blackpool South	LM	54	B1
Bedhampton	SO	11	C1		Blackrod	LM	54	C2
Bedminster	WR	8	B2		Blackwater	SO	11	A1
Bedwyn	WR	10	A1		Blaenau Ffestiniog	LM/FR	44	C1
Beeston	LM	47	C2		Blair Atholl	SC	78	B2
Bekesbourne	SO	13	A2		Blairhill	SC	72	A1
Belgrave & Birstall	ML	37	A2		Blakedown	LM	37	B1
Bellevue	ME	59	B2		Blake Hall	LT	32	B2
Belle Vue	LM	52	B1		Blake Street	LM	37	A2
Bellgrove	SC	76	B1		Blantyre	SC	76	C2
Bellingham	SO	18	A1		Blaydon	ER	69	B1
Bellshill	SC	72	B1		Bleasby	LM	48	B1

Station	Region	Page	Grid
Bletchley	LM	31	A1
Blue Anchor	WS	7	B2
Blundellsands & Crosby	LM	53	A1
Blythe Bridge	LM	46	C2
Blythswood (Proposed)	SC	76	B1
Boat of Garten	ST	78	A2
Bodmin Road	WR	2	B1
Bodorgan	LM	43	B2
Bognor Regis	SO	11	C1
Bogston	SC	71	A1
Boldon Colliery	ER	70	B1
Bolton	LM	55	C1
Bolton-on-Dearne	ER	56	C2
Bonar Bridge	SC	81	B2
Bond Street	LT	21	B1
Bookham	SO	11	A2
Boothferry Park*	ER	57	B2
Bootle (Cumbria)	LM	59	C2
Bootle New Strand	LM	53	A1
Bootle Oriel Road	LM	53	A1
Bordesley	LM	38	B2
Borough	LT	21	B2
Borough Green & Wrotham	SO	12	A2
Borth	LM	34	B2
Bosham	SO	11	C1
Boston	ER	49	C1
Boston Lodge	FR	43	C2
Boston Manor	LT	20	C1
Botley	SO	10	C2
Bottesford	ER	48	C1
Bounds Green	LT	23	C2
Bourne End	WR	31	C1
Bournemouth	SO	5	A2
Bourneville	LM	37	B2
Bow Brickhill	LM	31	A1
Bowes Park	ER	23	C2
Bowker Vale	LM	51	A2
Bowling	SC	75	A1
Bow Road	LT	22	B1
Boxhill & Westhumble	SO	11	A2
Bracknell	SO	11	A1
Bradford-on-Avon	WR	8	A1
Bradford Exchange	ER	56	B1
Bradford Forster Square	ER	56	B1
Brading	SO	6	A2
Braintree	ER	33	A1
Bramhall	LM	46	A1
Bramley	SO	10	A2
Brampton (Cumbria)	ER	66	C2
Brampton (Suffolk)	ER	42	B1
Branchton	SC	71	A1
Brandon	ER	41	B1
Branksome	SO	5	A2
Braystones	LM	59	B2
Bredbury	LM	52	C2
Breich	SC	72	B2
Brent Cross	LT	20	A2
Brentford Central	SO	20	C1
Brentwood	ER	32	C2
Bricket Wood	LM	31	B2
Bridgend	WR	27	C2
Bridge of Orchy	SC	78	B1
Bridge of Weir	SC	71	B2
Bridge Street	GG	76	B1
Bridgeton	SC	76	B1
Bridgwater	WR	8	B1
Bridgnorth	SV	37	B1
Bridlington	ER	57	A2
Brierfield	LM	55	B1
Brigg	ER	57	C2
Brighton	SO	12	C1
Brightside	ER	47	A1
Brimsdown	ER	24	B1
Brinnington	LM	52	C2
Bristol Parkway	WR	28	C2
Bristol Temple Meads	WR	8	B2
Brithdir	WR	28	B1
Brixton	SO/LT	21	C2
Broadbottom	LM	46	A2
Broad Green	LM	53	B2
Broadstairs	SO	14	A1
Broad Street	LM	21	B2
Brockenhurst	SO	10	C1
Brockholes	ER	56	C1
Brocklesby	ER	57	C2
Brockley	SO	22	C1
Bromborough	LM	45	A1
Bromley-by-Bow	LT	22	B1
Bromley Cross	LM	55	C1
Bromley North	SO	18	B2
Bromley South	SO	18	B2
Bromsgrove	WR	37	C2
Brondesbury	LM	21	B1
Brondesbury Park	LM	21	B1
Brooklands	LM	51	C2
Brookman's Park	ER	32	B1
Brookwood	SO	11	A2
Broome	WR	36	B2
Broomfleet	ER	57	B1
Brora	SC	81	B2
Brough	ER	57	B2
Broughty Ferry	SC	79	B1
Broxbourne	ER	32	B1
Bruce Grove	ER	23	C2
Brundall	ER	42	A1
Brundall Gardens	ER	42	A1
Bruton	WR	9	B1
Bryn	LM	54	C2
Brynglas	TL	34	A2
Buchanon Street	GG	76	B1
Buckenham	ER	42	A1
Buckfastleigh	DV	3	B1
Buckhurst Hill	LT	24	C2
Buckley	LM	45	B1
Bucknell	WR	36	B1
Bugle	WR	1	B2
Builth Road	LM	35	C2
Bungalow	ME	59	C1
Bures	ER	33	A1
Burgess Hill	SO	12	C1
Burley-in-Wharfedale	ER	56	A1
Burnage	LM	52	C1
Burneside	LM	60	C2
Burnham	WR	31	C1
Burnham-on-Crouch	ER	33	C1
Burnley Barracks	LM	55	B1
Burnley Central	LM	55	B1
Burnside	SC	76	C1
Burntisland	SC	73	A1
Burnt Oak	LT	31	C2
Burscough Bridge	LM	54	C2
Burscough Junction	LM	54	C2
Bursledon	SO	10	C2
Burton-on-Trent	LM	47	C1
Burton Joyce	LM	47	C2
Bury	LM	55	C1
Bury St. Edmunds	ER	41	C1
Busby	SC	76	C1
Bushey	LM/LT	31	C2
Bush Hill Park	ER	23	B2
Butlers Lane	LM	37	B2
Buxted	SO	12	B2
Buxton	LM	46	A2
Byfleet & New Haw	SO	15	C1
Bynea	WR	26	B2
Cabin	BF	54	B1
Cadoxton	WR	8	A1
Caergwrle	LM	45	B1
Caerphilly	WR	28	C1
Caersws	LM	35	B2
Caldicot	WR	28	C2
Caledonian Road	LT	21	A2

Station	Region	Page	Grid		Station	Region	Page	Grid
Caledonian Road & Barnsbury	LM	21	B2		Chatham	SO	13	A1
Calstock	WR	2	B2		Chathill	SC	74	A2
Camberley	SO	11	A1		Cheadle Hulme	LM	46	A1
Camborne	WR	1	C1		Cheam	SO	17	C1
Cambridge	ER	40	C1		Cheddington	LM	31	B1
Cambridge Heath	ER	22	B1		Chelford	LM	46	A1
Cambuslang	SC	76	C2		Chelmsford	ER	32	B2
Camden Road	LM	21	B1		Chelsfield	SO	12	A1
Camden Town	LT	21	B1		Cheltenham	WR	29	A2
Canley	LM	38	B1		Chepstow	WR	28	C2
Canning Town	ER	22	B1		Cherry Tree	LM	55	B1
Cannon Street	SO/LT	21	B2		Chertsey	SO	15	B1
Canonbury	LM	21	A2		Chesham	LT	31	B2
Canons Park	LT	31	C2		Cheshunt	ER	24	A1
Canterbury East	SO	13	A2		Chessington North	SO	16	C1
Canterbury West	SO	13	A2		Chessington South	SO	16	C1
Cantley	ER	42	A1		Chester	LM	45	B2
Capel Bangor	LM	33	B2		Chester-le-Street	ER	68	C1
Capenhurst	LM	45	A1		Chesterfield	ER	47	B1
Carbis Bay	WR	1	A1		Chester Road	LM	37	B2
Cardenden	SC	79	C1		Chestfield & Swalecliffe	SO	13	A2
Cardiff Bute Road	WR	28	C1		Chetnole	WR	8	C2
Cardiff Central	WR	28	C1		Chichester	SO	11	C1
Cardiff Queen Street	WR	28	C1		Chigwell	LT	24	C2
Cardonald	SC	75	B2		Chilham	SO	13	A2
Cardross	SC	71	A2		Chilworth & Albury	SO	11	B2
Carfin	SC	72	B1		Chingford	ER	24	C1
Cargo Fleet	ER	62	B2		Chinley	LM	46	A2
Cark & Cartmel	LM	60	C1		Chippenham	WR	29	C2
Carlisle	LM	66	C2		Chipstead	SO	12	A1
Carlton	LM	47	C2		Chirk	LM	45	C1
Carluke	SC	72	B2		Chislehurst	SO	18	B2
Carmarthen	WR	26	B2		Chiswick	SO	20	C2
Carnforth	LM	60	C2		Chiswick Park	LT	20	C2
Carnoustie	SC	79	B1		Cholsey	WR	30	C2
Carntyne	SC	76	B2		Chorley	LM	54	C2
Carpenders Park	LM/LT	31	C2		Chorleywood	LM/LT	31	C2
Carr Bridge	SC	78	A2		Christ's Hospital	SO	11	B2
Carshalton	SO	17	B1		Christchurch	SU	5	A2
Carshalton Beeches	SO	17	C1		Church & Ostwaldwhistle	LM	55	B1
Carstairs	SC	72	B2		Church Fenton	ER	56	B2
Cartsdyke	SC	71	A1		Church Stretton	LM	36	B2
Castle Bar Park	WR	20	B1		Churston	TD	3	B2
Castle Caereinon	WL	36	A1		Cilmery	LM	35	C2
Castle Cary	WR	8	B2		Clacton	ER	33	B2
Castleford	ER	56	B2		Clandon	SO	11	A2
Castleton	LM	55	C1		Clapham	SO	21	C2
Castleton Moor	ER	63	B1		Clapham (Yorks.)	LM	55	A1
Castletown	MS	59	C1		Clapham Common	LT	21	C2
Caterham	SO	12	A1		Clapham Junction	SO	21	C1
Catford	SO	18	A1		Clapham North	LT	21	C2
Catford Bridge	SO	18	A1		Clapham South	LT	17	A1
Cathcart	SC	76	C1		Clapton	ER	22	A1
Cattal	ER	56	A2		Clarbeston Road	WR	25	A2
Causeland	WR	2	B1		Clarkston	SC	76	C1
Cefn-y-Bedd	LM	45	B1		Claverdon	LM	38	C1
Cefn On	WR	28	C1		Claygate	SO	16	C1
Cei Llydan	LL	43	B2		Clayton West	ER	56	C1
Cessnock	GG	75	B2		Cleethorpes	ER	58	C1
Chadwell Heath	ER	32	C2		Cleland	SC	72	B1
Chalfont & Latimer	LM/LT	31	C2		Cleveleys	BF	54	B1
Chalk Farm	LT	21	B1		Clifton	LM	51	A2
Chalkwell	ER	33	C1		Clifton Down	WR	8	A2
Chancery Lane	LT	21	B2		Clock House	SO	18	B1
Chapel-en-le-Frith	LM	46	A2		Clogwyn	SM	43	B2
Chapelton	WR	6	B2		Clydebank	SC	75	A1
Chapeltown	ER	47	A1		Clynderwen	WR	26	B1
Chappel & Wakes Colne	ER	33	A1		Coatbridge Central	SC	72	B1
Charing	SO	13	A1		Coatbridge Sunnyside	SC	72	B1
Charing Cross (Glasgow)	SC	76	B1		Coatdyke	SC	72	B1
Charing Cross (London)	SO/LT	21	B2		Cobham & Stoke d'Abernon	SO	11	A2
Charlbury	WR	30	B1		Cockfosters	LT	23	B1
Charlton	SO	22	C2		Codsall	LM	37	A1
Chartham	SO	13	A2		Cogan	WR	8	A1
Chassen Road	LM	51	C1		Colchester	ER	33	A1

Station	Region	Page	Grid
Colindale	LT	31	C2
Collier's Wood	LT	17	A1
Collingham	ER	48	B1
Collington	SO	12	C2
Colne	LM	55	B1
Colwall	WR	29	A1
Colwyn Bay	LM	44	A1
Colyford	ST	4	A1
Colyton	ST	4	A1
Combe (Oxon)	WR	30	B1
Commondale	ER	63	B1
Congleton	LM	46	B1
Conisborough	ER	56	C2
Connel Ferry	SC	77	B2
Cooden Beach	SO	12	C2
Cookham	WR	31	C1
Cooksbridge	SO	12	C1
Coombe (Cornwall)	WR	2	B1
Coombe Road	SO	17	C2
Copland Road	GG	75	B2
Copplestone	WR	7	C1
Corbridge	ER	67	C2
Corkerhill	SC	75	B2
Corkickle	LM	59	B2
Cornaa	ME	59	B2
Corpach	SC	78	B1
Corrour	SC	78	B1
Coryton	WR	28	C1
Coseley	LM	37	B2
Cosford	LM	37	A1
Cosham	SO	10	C2
Cottingham	ER	57	B2
Coulsdon North	SO	12	A1
Coulsdon South	SO	12	A1
Covent Garden	LT	21	B2
Coventry	LM	38	B1
Cowcaddens	GG	76	B1
Cowden	SO	12	B2
Cowdenbeath	SC	73	A1
Cradley	LM	37	B2
Craigendoran	SC	71	A1
Cramlington	ER	68	B1
Craven Arms	WR	36	B2
Crawley	SO	12	B1
Crayford	SO	32	C2
Crediton	WR	3	A1
Cressing	ER	33	B1
Cressington	LM	53	C2
Crewe	LM	46	B1
Crewkerne	WR	8	C2
Crews Hill	ER	23	A2
Crianlarich	SC	78	C1
Criccieth	LM	43	C2
Cricklewood	LM	20	A2
Croftfoot	SC	76	C1
Crofton Park	SO	18	A1
Cromer	ER	50	C1
Cromford	LM	47	B1
Crookston	SC	75	B2
Cross Gates	ER	56	B1
Crosshill	SC	76	C1
Crossmyloof	SC	75	C2
Croston	LM	54	C2
Crouch Hill	ER	21	A2
Crowborough & Jarvis Brook	SO	12	B2
Crowle	ER	57	C1
Crowthorne	SO	11	A1
Croxley	LT	31	C2
Croxley Green	LM	31	C2
Croy	SC	72	A1
Crumpsall	LM	52	A1
Crystal Palace	SO	17	A2
Cuddington	LM	45	A2
Cuffley	ER	23	A2
Culham	WR	30	C2
Cullercoats	ER	70	A2
Culrain	SC	81	B2
Cumbernauld	SC	72	A1
Cupar	SC	79	C1
Custom House	ER	22	B2
Cuxton	SO	12	A2
Cyfronydd	WL	36	A1
Cynghordy	WR	27	A1
Dagenham Dock	ER	32	C2
Dagenham East	LT	32	C2
Dagenham Heathway	LT	32	C2
Daisy Hill	LM	55	C1
Dalegarth	RE	60	B1
Dalmally	SC	78	C1
Dalmarnock	SC	76	B1
Dalmeny	SC	73	A1
Dalmuir	SC	75	A1
Dalreoch	SC	71	A2
Dalry	SC	71	B1
Dalston (Cumbria)	LM	66	C2
Dalston Junction	LM	21	C1
Dalton	LM	60	C1
Dalwhinnie	SC	78	A2
Damems	KW	55	B2
Danby	ER	63	B1
Dane Road	LM	51	C2
Danzey	LM	37	C2
Darlington	ER	62	B1
Darnall	ER	47	A1
Darsham	ER	42	C1
Dartford	SO	32	C2
Darton	ER	56	C1
Darwen	LM	55	B1
Datchet	SO	31	C2
Davenport	LM	52	C1
Dawlish	WR	3	A2
Dawlish Warren	WR	3	A2
Dduallt	FR	44	C1
Deal	SO	14	A1
Dean	SO	10	B1
Dean Lane	LM	52	A1
Deansgate	LM	51	B2
Debden	LT	24	B2
Deepdene	SO	11	A2
Deganwy	LM	44	A1
Delamere	LM	45	B2
Denby Dale	ER	56	C1
Denham	LM	19	A1
Denham Golf Club	LM	31	C2
Denmark Hill	SO	21	C2
Dent*	LM	61	C1
Denton	LM	52	B2
Deptford	SO	22	C1
Derby	LM	47	C1
Derby Castle (Douglas)	ME	59	C1
Derby Road (Ipswich)	ER	33	A2
Devil's Bridge	LM	34	B2
Devonport	WR	2	B2
Dewsbury	ER	56	B1
Dhoon	ME	59	C2
Didcot	WR	30	C2
Dilton Marsh	SO	9	A1
Dinas Powis	WR	8	A1
Dinas Rhondda	WR	27	C2
Dingle Road	WR	8	A1
Dingwall	SC	81	C2
Dinsdale	ER	62	B1
Dinting	LM	46	A2
Disley	LM	46	A2
Diss	ER	41	B2
Ditton	LM	45	A2
Dockyard	WR	2	B2
Dolau	WR	36	C1

Heniarth	WL	35	A2		Hounslow East	LT	20	C1
Henley-in-Arden	LM	37	C2		Hounslow West	LT	19	C2
Henley-on-Thames	WR	31	C1		Houston	SC	71	B2
Hensall	ER	56	B2		Hove	SO	12	C1
Hereford	WR	28	A2		Howden	ER	57	B1
Herne Bay	SO	13	A2		Howden-on-Tyne	ER	70	B1
Herne Hill	SO	17	A2		Howstrake	ME	59	C2
Hersham	SO	15	B2		Hoylake	LM	45	A1
Hertford East	ER	32	B1		Hubbert's Bridge	ER	49	C1
Hertford North	ER	32	B1		Huddersfield	ER	55	C2
Hessle	ER	57	B2		Hull	ER	57	B2
Heswall	LM	45	A1		Huncoat	LM	55	B1
Hever	SO	12	B1		Hungerford	WR	10	A1
Hexham	ER	67	C2		Hunmanby	ER	63	C2
Heyford	WR	30	A2		Huntingdon	ER	40	C1
Higham	SO	32	C2		Huntly	SC	82	C1
Highams Park	ER	24	C1		Hunt's Cross	LM	45	A2
High Barnet	LT	23	B1		Hurst Green	SO	12	A1
Highbridge	WR	8	B1		Hutton Cranswick	ER	57	A2
High Brooms	SO	12	B2		Huyton	LM	45	A2
Highbury & Islington	ER/LT	21	A2		Hyde Central	LM	52	B2
Highgate	LT	21	A1		Hyde North	LM	52	B2
Highley	SV	37	B1		Hyde Park Corner	LT	21	B1
High Shields	ER	70	B2		Hykeham	ER	48	B2
High Street (Glasgow)	SC	76	B1		Hyndland	SC	75	B2
High Street, Kensington	LT	21	C1		Hythe (Essex)	ER	33	A2
Hightown	LM	54	C1		Hythe (Kent)	RH	13	B2
High Wycombe	LM	31	C1		Ickenham	LT	19	A1
Hildenborough	SO	12	A2		Ifield	SO	12	B1
Hillfoot	SC	75	A2		Ilford	ER	22	A2
Hillhead	GG	75	B2		Ilkley	ER	55	A2
Hillingdon	LT	19	A1		Ince	LM	54	C2
Hillington East	SC	75	B2		Ince & Elton	LM	45	A2
Hillington West	SC	75	B2		Ingatestone	ER	32	B2
Hillside	LM	54	C1		Ingrow	KW	55	B2
Hilsea	SO	10	C2		Insch	SC	82	C2
Hinchley Wood	SO	16	B1		Invergordon	SC	81	C2
Hinckley	LM	38	B2		Invergowrie	SC	79	B1
Hindley	LM	54	C2		Inverkeithing	SC	73	A1
Hinton Admiral	SO	6	A1		Inverkip	SC	71	A1
Hitchin	ER	31	A2		Inverness	SC	81	C2
Hither Green	SO	18	AT		Invershin	SC	81	B2
Hockley	ER	33	C1		Inverurie	SC	79	A2
Holborn	LT	21	B2		Ipswich	ER	33	A2
Holborn Viaduct	SO	21	B2		Irlam	LM	51	C1
Holland Park	LT	21	B1		Irton Road	RE	60	B1
Hollingbourne	SO	13	A1		Irvine	SC	71	C2
Hollinwood	LM	52	A1		Isleworth	SO	20	C1
Holloway Road	LT	21	A2		Iver	WR	19	B1
Holmes Chapel	LM	46	B1		Jarrow	ER	70	B1
Holmwood	SO	11	B2		Jesmond	ER	69	B2
Holton Heath	SO	5	A2		Johnston	WR	25	B2
Holyhead	LM	43	A1		Johnstone	SC	71	B2
Holytown	SC	72	B1		Jordanhill	SC	75	B2
Honiton	WR	8	C1		Kearsley	LM	51	A1
Honley	ER	55	C2		Kearsney	SO	14	B1
Honor Oak Park	SO	18	A1		Keighley	ER/KW	55	B2
Hook	SO	11	A1		Keith Junction	SC	82	C1
Hoo Staff Halt*	SO	32	C2		Kelvedon	ER	33	B1
Hooton	LM	45	A1		Kelvin Bridge	GG	76	B1
Hope (Clwyd)	LM	45	B1		Kelvin Hall	GG	75	B2
Hope (Derbyshire)	LM	47	A1		Kemble	WR	29	C2
Hopton Heath	WR	36	B1		Kempston Hardwick	LM	31	A2
Horley	SO	12	B1		Kempton Park*	SO	15	A2
Hornchurch	LT	32	C2		Kemsing	SO	12	A2
Hornsey	ER	21	A2		Kemsley	SO	13	A1
Horsforth	ER	56	B1		Kemsley Down	SK	13	A1
Horsham	SO	11	B2		Kendal	LM	60	C2
Horsley	SO	11	A2		Kenley	SO	17	C2
Horstead Keynes	BL	12	B1		Kennett	ER	40	C2
Horton*	LM	61	C1		Kennington	LT	21	C2
Hoscar	LM	54	C2		Kennishead	SC	75	C2
Hough Green	LM	45	A2		Kensal Green	LM/LT	20	B2
Hounslow	SO	20	C1		Kensal Rise	LM	20	B2
Hounslow Central	LT	19	C2		Kensington Olympia	LM/LT	21	C1

Station	Region	Page	Grid	Station	Region	Page	Grid
Kent House	SO	18	A1	Langbank	SC	71	A2
Kentish Town	LM	21	A1	Langley	WR	31	C2
Kenton	LM/LT	20	A1	Langley Green	LM	37	B2
Kents Bank	LM	60	C2	Langside	SC	76	C1
Kettering for Corby	LM	39	B1	Langwathby*	LM	60	A2
Kew Bridge	SO	20	C2	Lapford	WR	7	C1
Kew Gardens	SO/LT	20	C2	Lapworth	LM	38	C1
Keyham	WR	2	B2	Larbert	SC	72	A2
Keynsham	WR	9	A1	Largs	SC	71	B1
Kidbrooke	SO	22	C2	Latimer Road	LT	20	B2
Kidderminster	LM	37	B1	Lawrence Hill	WR	8	A2
Kidsgrove	LM	46	B2	Laxey	ME	59	C2
Kidwelly	WR	26	B2	Layton	LM	54	B1
Kilburn	LT	21	A1	Lazonby*	LM	60	A2
Kilburn High Road	LM	21	B1	Lea Bridge	ER	22	A1
Kilburn Park	LT	21	B1	Leagrave	LM	31	A2
Kildale	ER	62	B2	Lea Hall	LM	37	B2
Kildonan	SC	81	B2	Lealholm	ER	63	B1
Kilgetty	WR	26	B1	Leamington Spa	LM	38	C1
Kilmacolm	SC	71	A2	Leasowe	LM	45	A1
Kilmarnock	SC	71	C2	Leatherhead	SO	11	A2
Kilpatrick	SC	75	A1	Ledbury	WR	29	A1
Kilwinning	SC	71	B1	Lee	SO	18	A2
Kinbrace	SC	81	A2	Leeds	ER	56	B1
King's Langley	LM	31	B2	Leicester	LM	38	A2
King's Lynn	ER	40	A2	Leicester Square	LT	21	B2
King's Norton	LM	37	B2	Leigh	SO	12	B2
King's Nympton	WR	7	C1	Leigh-on-Sea	ER	33	C1
King's Park	SC	76	C1	Leighton Buzzard	LM	31	A1
King's Sutton	LM	30	A2	Lelant	WR	1	A1
Kingham	WR	30	B1	Lenham	SO	13	A1
Kinghorn	SC	73	A1	Lenzie	SC	76	A2
Kingsbury	LT	20	A2	Leominster	WR	36	C2
Kings Cross	ER/LT	21	B2	Letchworth	ER	32	A1
Kingsknowe	SC	73	A1	Leuchars	SC	79	C1
Kingston	SO	16	B1	Levenshulme	LM	52	C1
Kingswear	TD	3	B2	Levisham	NY	63	C1
Kingswood & Burgh Heath	SO	12	A1	Lewaigue	ME	59	B2
Kingussie	SC	78	A2	Lewes	SO	12	C1
Kinning Park	GG	75	B2	Lewisham	SO	22	C1
Kintbury	WR	10	A1	Leyland	LM	54	B2
Kirby Cross	ER	33	B2	Leyton	LT	22	A1
Kirkby (Merseyside)	LM	53	A2	Leyton Midland Road	FR	22	A1
Kirkby-in-Furness	LM	60	C1	Leytonstone	LT	22	A1
Kirkby Stephen*	LM	61	B1	Leytonstone High Road	ER	22	A1
Kirkcaldy	SC	73	A1	Lichfield City	LM	37	A2
Kirkconnel	SC	63	A1	Lichfield Trent Valley	LM	37	A2
Kirkdale	LM	53	B1	Lidlington	LM	31	A2
Kirkham & Wesham	LM	54	B2	Lincoln Central	ER	48	B2
Kirkhill	SC	76	C2	Lincoln St. Marks	ER	48	B2
Kirton Lindsey	ER	57	C2	Lingfield	SO	12	B1
Kiveton Bridge	ER	47	A2	Linlithgow	SC	72	A2
Kiveton Park	ER	47	A2	Liphook	SO	11	B1
Knaresborough	ER	56	A1	Liskeard	WR	2	B1
Knebworth	ER	32	B1	Liss	SO	11	B1
Knighton	WR	36	C1	Little Bispham	BF	54	B1
Knightsbridge	LT	21	C1	Littleborough	LM	55	C2
Knockholt	SO	12	A2	Littlehampton	SO	11	C2
Knottingley	ER	56	B2	Littlehaven	SO	11	B2
Knucklas	WR	36	B1	Little Kimble	LM	31	B1
Knutsford	LM	46	A1	Littleport	ER	40	B2
Kyle of Lochalsh	SC	80	C2	Little Sutton	LM	45	A1
Ladbroke Grove	LT	21	B1	Liverpool Central	LM	53	B1
Lade Halt	RH	13	C2	Liverpool James Street	LM	53	B1
Ladybank	SC	79	C1	Liverpool Lime Street	LM	53	B1
Ladywell	SO	22	C1	Liverpool Moorfields	LM	53	B1
Laindon	ER	32	C2	Liverpool Street (London)	ER/LT	21	B2
Lairg	SC	81	B2	Llanaber	LM	34	A2
Lakenheath	ER	40	B2	Llanbadarn	LM	34	B2
Lakeside	LH	60	C1	Llanbedr & Pensarn	LM	43	C2
Lambeth North	LT	21	C2	Llanberis	SM	43	B2
Lamphey	WR	25	B2	Llanbister Road	WR	36	C1
Lanark	SC	72	C2	Llanbradach	WR	28	C1
Lancaster	LM	54	A2	Llandaff for Whitchurch	WR	28	C1
Lancaster Gate	LT	21	B1	Llandanwg	LM	43	C2
Lancing	SO	11	C2	Llandecwyn	LM	44	C1

Llandeilo	WR	27	A1
Llandovery	WR	27	A1
Llandrindod Wells	LM	35	C2
Llandudno	LM	44	A1
Llandudno Junction	LM	44	A1
Llandudno Victoria	GO	44	A1
Llandbie	WR	27	B1
Llanelli	WR	26	B2
Llanfair Caereinon	WL	35	A2
Llanfairfechan	LM	44	A1
Llanfairswll	LM	43	A2
Llangadog	WR	27	A1
Llangammarch Wells	WR	27	A2
Llangelynin	LM	33	A2
Llangennech	WR	26	B2
Llangower	BA	44	C2
Llangunllo	WR	36	B1
Llanishen	WR	28	C1
Llanuwchllyn	BA	44	C2
Llanrwst	LM	44	B1
Llanwrda	WR	27	A1
Llanwrtyd Wells	WR	27	A2
Llwyngwril	LM	34	A2
Llwynpia	WR	27	C2
Llyn Ystradau	FR	44	C1
Lochailort	SC	77	A2
Locheilside	SC	78	A1
Lochgelly	SC	79	C1
Lochluichart	SC	81	C1
Lochside	SC	71	B2
Lockerbie	SC	66	B1
Lockwood	ER	55	C2
London Bridge	SO/LT	21	B2
London Fields	ER	22	B1
London Road (Brighton)	SO	12	C1
London Road (Guildford)	SO	11	A2
Longbenton	ER	69	A2
Longbridge	LM	37	B2
Long Buckby	LM	38	C2
Longcross	SO	11	A2
Long Eaton	LM	47	C2
Longfield	SO	12	A2
Longniddry	SC	73	A2
Longport	LM	46	B1
Long Preston	LM	55	A1
Longton	LM	46	C2
Looe	WR	2	B1
Lostwithiel	WR	2	B1
Loughborough	LM	38	A2
Loughborough Central	ML	38	A2
Loughborough Junction	SO	21	C2
Loughton	LT	24	B2
Lowdham	LM	47	C2
Lower Edmonton	ER	23	C2
Lower Sydenham	SO	18	A1
Lowestoft	ER	42	B2
Ludlow	WR	36	B2
Luton	LM	31	B2
Luxulyan	WR	1	B2
Lydney	WR	28	B2
Lye	LM	37	B2
Lymington Pier	SO	6	A1
Lymington Town	SO	6	A1
Lympstone	WR	3	A2
Lympstone Commando	WR	3	A2
Lyndhurst Road	SO	10	C1.
Lytham	LM	54	B1
Macclesfield	LM	46	A2
Machynlleth	LM	34	A2
Maddieson's Camp	RH	13	C2
Magdalen Road	ER	40	A2
Maghull	LM	54	C2
Maida Vale	LT	21	B1
Maidenhead	WR	31	C1
Maiden Newton	WR	4	A2

Maidstone Barracks	SO	13	A1
Maidstone East	SO	13	A1
Maidstone West	SO	13	A1
Malden Manor	SO	16	B2
Mallaig	SC	77	A2
Malton	ER	63	C1
Malvern Link	WR	37	C1
Manchester Oxford Road	LM	52	B1
Manchester Piccadilly	LM	52	B1
Manchester Square	BF	54	B1
Manchester United Football Ground*	LM	51	B2
Manchester Victoria	LM	52	B1
Manea	ER	40	B2
Manningtree	ER	33	A2
Manorbier	WR	25	B2
Manor House	LT	21	A2
Manor Park	ER	22	A2
Manor Road	LM	45	A1
Manors	ER	69	B2
Mansion House	LT	21	B2
Marble Arch	LT	21	B1
March	ER	40	B1
Marden	SO	13	B1
Margate	SO	14	A1
Market Harborough	LM	39	B1
Market Rasen	ER	48	A2
Markinch for Glenrothes	SC	79	C1
Marks Tey	ER	33	A1
Marlow	WR	31	C1
Marple	LM	52	C2
Marsden	ER	55	C2
Marske	ER	62	A2
Marston Green	LM	38	B1
Martin Mill	SO	14	B1
Maryland	ER	22	A1
Marylebone	LM/LT	21	B1
Maryport	LM	59	A2
Matlock	LM	47	B1
Matlock Bath	LM	47	B1
Mauldeth Road	LM	52	C1
Maxwell Park	SC	75	B2
Maybole	SC	64	A1
Maze Hill	SO	22	C1
Meldreth	ER	32	A1
Melton*	ER	57	B2
Melton Mowbray	LM	39	A1
Menheniot	WR	2	B1
Menston	ER	56	B1
Meols	LM	45	A1
Meols Cop	LM	54	C1
Meopham	SO	12	A2
Merstham	SO	12	A1
Merthyr	WR	27	B2
Merthyr Vale	WR	27	B2
Merton Park	SO	17	A1
Metheringham	ER	48	B2
Mexborough	ER	56	C2
Micheldever	SO	10	B2
Micklefield	ER	56	B2
Midcalder	SC	73	B1
Middlesborough	ER	62	B2
Middlewood	LM	46	A2
Midgham	WR	10	A2
Mile End	LT	22	B1
Miles Platting	LM	52	B1
Milford (Surrey)	SO	11	B2
Milford Haven	WR	25	B2
Millbrook (Beds)	LM	31	A2
Millbrook (Hants)	SO	10	C1
Mill Hill (Lancs)	LM	55	B1
Mill Hill Broadway	LM	31	C2
Mill Hill East	LT	23	C1
Millom	LM	60	C1
Miingavie	SC	75	A2

Station	Region	Page	Grid
Milnrow	LM	55	C2
Minehead	WS	7	B2
Minffordd	LM/FR	43	C2
Minorca	ME	59	C2
Minster	SO	14	A1
Mirfield	ER	56	C1
Mistley	ER	33	A2
Mitcham	SO	17	B1
Mitcham Junction	SO	17	B1
Mobberley	LM	46	A1
Monifieth	SC	79	B1
Monkseaton	ER	70	A1
Monks Risborough	LM	31	B1
Montpelier	WR	8	A2
Montrose	SC	79	B2
Monument	LT	21	B2
Moorgate	ER/LT	21	B2
Moor Park	LM/LT	31	C2
Moorside	LM	51	A1
Moorthorpe	ER	56	C2
Morar	SC	77	A2
Morchard Road	WR	7	C1
Morden	LT	17	B1
Morden Road	SO	17	B1
Morden South	SO	17	B1
Morecambe	LM	54	A2
Moreton (Dorset)	SO	5	A1
Moreton (Merseyside)	LM	45	A1
Moreton-in-Marsh	WR	30	A1
Morfa Mawddach	LM	34	A2
Morley	ER	56	B1
Mornington Crescent	LT	21	B1
Morpeth	ER	68	B1
Mortimer	SO	10	A2
Mortlake	SO	20	C2
Moses Gate	LM	51	A1
Mossley	LM	55	C2
Mossley Hill	LM	53	C2
Mosspark	SC	75	B2
Moston	LM	52	A1
Motherwell	SC	72	B1
Motspur Park	SO	16	B2
Mottingham	SO	18	A2
Mottram Staff Halt*	LM	46	A2
Mouldsworth	LM	45	B2
Mount Florida	SC	76	C1
Muirend	SC	76	C1
Muir of Ord	SC	81	C1
Muncaster Mill	RE	59	B2
Mytholmroyd	ER	55	B2
Nafferton	ER	57	A2
Nailsea and Backwell	WR	8	A2
Nairn	SC	81	C2
Nant Gwernol	TL	34	A2
Nantwich	LM	46	B2
Nantyronen	LM	34	B2
Narberth	WR	26	B1
Narborough	LM	38	A2
Navigation Road	LM	51	C2
Neasden	LT	20	A2
Neath	WR	27	C1
Needham Market	ER	41	C2
Neilston	SC	75	C1
Nelson	LM	55	B1
Neston	LM	45	A1
Netherfield	LM	47	C2
Netherton	LM	59	B2
Netley	SO	10	C2
Newark Castle	ER	48	B1
Newark Northgate	ER	48	B1
New Barnet	ER	23	B1
New Beckenham	SO	18	A1
New Brighton	LM	53	B1
Newbury	WR	10	A2
Newbury Park	LT	22	A2
Newbury Racecourse*	WR	10	A2
Newby Bridge	LH	60	C1
Newcastle	ER	69	B2
New Clee	ER	58	C1
New Cross	SO/LT	22	C1
New Cross Gate	SO/LT	22	C1
New Eltham	SO	18	A2
New Hadley	LM	37	A1
Newhaven Harbour	SO	12	C1
Newhaven Town	SO	12	C1
New Hey	LM	55	C2
New Holland Pier	ER	57	B2
New Holland Town	ER	57	B2
New Hythe	SO	12	A2
Newington	SO	13	A1
New Lane	LM	54	C2
New Malden	SO	16	B2
Newmarket	ER	40	C2
New Mills Central	LM	46	A2
New Mills Newtown	LM	46	A2
New Milton	SO	6	A1
Newport (Essex)	ER	32	A2
Newport (Gwent)	WR	28	C1
New Pudsey	ER	56	B1
Newquay	WR	1	B2
New Romney	RH	13	B2
New Southgate	ER	23	C1
Newton (Greater Glasgow)	SC	76	C2
Newton (Greater Manchester)	LM	52	B2
Newton-le-Willows	LM	45	A2
Newton-on-Ayr	SC	71	C2
Newton Abbot	WR	3	B2
Newton Aycliffe	ER	62	A1
Newtonmore	SC	78	A2
Newton St. Cyres	WR	3	A1
Newtown	LM	35	B2
Ninian Park*	WR	28	C1
Nitshill	SC	75	C2
Norbiton	SO	16	B2
Norbury	SO	17	B2
Norman's Bay	SO	12	C2
Normanton	ER	56	B1
North Acton	LT	20	B2
Northallerton	ER	62	C1
Northampton	LM	39	C1
North Berwick	SC	73	A2
North Camp	SO	11	A1
North Dulwich	SO	17	A2
North Ealing	LT	20	B2
Northfield	LM	37	B2
Northfields	LT	20	C1
North Filton Platform*	WR	28	C2
Northfleet	SO	32	C2
North Harrow	LT	19	A2
Northolt	LT	19	B2
Northolt Park	LM	20	A1
North Queensferry	SC	73	A1
North Road	ER	62	B1
North Sheen	SO	20	C2
North Shields	ER	70	A1
Northumberland Park	ER	24	C1
North Walsham	ER	50	C2
North Weald	LT	32	B2
North Wembley	LM/LT	20	A1
Northwich	LM	46	A1
Northwick Park	LT	20	A1
Northwood (Greater London)	LT	31	C2
Northwood (Worcs)	SV	37	B1
Northwood Hills	LT	31	C2
North Woolwich	ER	22	B2
Norton Bridge	LM	46	C1
Norwich	ER	41	A2
Norwood Junction	SO	17	B2

Nottingham	LM	47	C2
Notting Hill Gate	LT	21	B1
Nuneaton	LM	38	B1
Nunhead	SO	22	C1
Nunthorpe	ER	62	B2
Nutfield	SO	12	A1
Nutbourne	SO	11	C1
Oakengates	LM	37	A1
Oakham	LM	39	A1
Oakleigh Park	ER	23	B1
Oakwood	LT	23	B2
Oakworth	KW	55	B2
Oban	SC	77	B2
Ockendon	ER	32	C2
Ockley & Capel	SO	11	B2
Oldbury	LM	37	B2
Oldfield Park	WR	9	A1
Oldham Mumps	LM	52	A2
Oldham Werneth	LM	52	A2
Old Hill	LM	37	B2
Old Roan	LM	53	A2
Old Street	ER/LT	21	B2
Old Trafford	LM	51	B2
Olton	LM	37	B2
Onchan Head	ME	59	C1
Ongar	LT	32	B2
Ore	SO	13	C1
Ormesby	ER	62	B2
Ormskirk	LM	54	C2
Orpington	SO	12	A1
Orrell	LM	54	C2
Orrell Park	LM	53	A2
Orton Mere	NV	39	A2
Osterley	LT	20	C1
Otford	SO	12	A2
Oulton Broad North	ER	42	B2
Oulton Broad South	ER	42	B2
Oval	LT	21	C2
Overton	SO	10	A2
Oxenholme	LM	60	C2
Oxenhope	KW	55	B2
Oxford	WR	30	B2
Oxford Circus	LT	21	B1
Oxshott	SO	16	C1
Oxted	SO	12	A1
Paddington	WR/LT	21	B1
Paddock Wood	SO	12	B2
Padgate	LM	45	A2
Paignton	WR/TD	3	B2
Paisley Canal	SC	75	B1
Paisley Gilmour Street	SC	75	B1
Paisley St. James	SC	75	B1
Palmers Green	ER	23	C2
Pangbourne	WR	30	C2
Pannal	ER	56	A1
Pantyffynon	WR	27	B1
Par	WR	2	B1
Parbold	LM	54	C2
Park	LM	52	B1
Park Royal	LT	20	B2
Parkstone	SO	5	A2
Park Street	LM	31	B2
Parsons Green	LT	21	C1
Parson Street	WR	8	B2
Partick	SC/GG	75	B2
Parton	LM	59	B2
Patchway	WR	28	C2
Patricroft	LM	51	B1
Patterton	SC	75	C2
Peartree	LM	47	C1
Peckham Rye	SO	21	C2
Pegswood	ER	68	B1
Pelaw	ER	70	B1
Pemberton	LM	54	C2
Pembrey & Burry Port	WR	26	B2
Pembroke	WR	25	B2
Pembroke Dock	WR	25	B2
Penally	WR	26	B1
Penarth	WR	8	A1
Pendleton	LM	51	B2
Pengam	WR	28	C1
Penge East	SO	18	A1
Penge West	SO	18	A1
Penhelig	LM	34	B2
Penistone	ER	56	C1
Penkridge	LM	37	A2
Penmaenmawr	LM	44	A1
Penmere	WR	1	C1
Penrhyn (Gwynedd)	FR	44	C1
Penrhyndeudraeth	LM	44	C1
Penrith	LM	60	A2
Penryn (Cornwall)	WE	1	C1
Penshurst	SO	12	B2
Pentrebach	WR	27	B2
Penybont	LM	35	C2
Penychain	LM	43	C2
Penyffordd	LM	45	B1
Penzance	WR	1	A1
Percy Main	ER	70	B1
Perivale	LT	20	B1
Perranwell	WR	1	C1
Perry Barr	LM	37	B2
Pershore	WR	37	C2
Perth	SC	79	C1
Peterborough	ER	39	A2
Petersfield	SO	11	B1
Petts Wood	SO	18	B2
Pevensey & Westham	SO	12	C2
Pevensey Bay	SO	12	C2
Pewsey	WR	9	A2
Piccadilly Circus	LT	21	B2
Pickering	NY	63	C1
Pilning	WR	28	C2
Pimlico	LT	21	C2
Pinner	LT	19	A2
Pitlochry	SC	78	B2
Pitsea	ER	33	C1
Plaistow	LT	22	B2
Pleasington	LM	54	B2
Pleasure Beach	BF	54	B1
Plockton	SC	80	C2
Pluckley	SO	13	B1
Plumley	LM	46	A1
Plumpton	SO	12	C1
Plumstead	SO	22	C2
Plymouth	WR	2	B2
Pokesdown	SO	5	A2
Polegate	SO	12	C2
Polesworth	LM	38	A1
Pollokshaws East	SC	75	C2
Pollokshaws West	SC	75	C2
Pollokshields East	SC	76	B1
Pollokshields West	SC	76	B1
Polmont	SC	72	A2
Polsloe Bridge	WR	3	A2
Ponders End	ER	24	B1
Pontardulais	WR	26	B2
Pontefract Baghill	ER	56	B2
Pontefract Monkhill	ER	56	B2
Pontlottyn	WR	27	B2
Pont-y-Pant	LM	44	B1
Pontypool	WR	28	B1
Pontypridd	WR	27	C2
Poole	SO	5	A2
Poppleton	ER	56	A2
Portchester	SO	10	C2
Port Erin	MS	59	C1
Port Glasgow	SC	71	A2
Porth	WR	27	C2
Porthmadog	LM/FR	43	C2

Portslade & West Hove	SO	12	C1		Redditch	LM	37	C2
Portsmouth & Southsea	SO	10	C2		Redhill	SO	12	A1
Portsmouth Arms	WR	7	C1		Redland	WR	8	A2
Portsmouth Harbour	SO	10	C2		Redruth	WR	1	C1
Port Soderick	MS	59	C1		Reedham (Norfolk)	ER	42	A1
Port St. Mary	MS	59	C1		Reedham (Surrey)	SO	17	C2
Port Sunlight	LM	53	C1		Regent's Park	LT	21	B1
Port Talbot	WR	27	C1		Reigate	SO	12	A1
Potters Bar	ER	23	A1		Renton	SC	71	A2
Poulton-le-Fylde	LM	54	B1		Retford	ER	48	A1
Poynton	LM	46	A2		Rheidol Falls	LM	34	B2
Prees	LM	45	C2		Rhiwbina	WR	28	C1
Prescot	LM	45	A2		Rhiwfron	LM	34	B2
Prestatyn	LM	44	A2		Rhosneigr	LM	43	A1
Prestbury	LM	46	A2		Rhydyronen	TL	34	A2
Prestbury Park (Racecourse)*	WR	29	A2		Rhyl	LM	44	A2
Preston	LM	54	B2		Rhymney	WR	27	B2
Prestonpans	SC	73	A2		Ribblehead*	LM	61	C1
Preston Park	SO	12	C1		Richmond	SO/LT	20	C1
Preston Road (Greater London)	LT	20	A1		Rickmansworth	LM/LT	31	C2
Preston Road (Merseyside)	LM	53	A2		Riddlesdown	SO	17	C2
Prestwich	LM	51	A2		Ridgmont	LM	31	A2
Prestwick	SC	71	C2		Riding Mill	ER	67	C2
Primrose Hill	LM	21	B1		Rishton	LM	55	B1
Princes Risborough	LM	31	B1		Robertsbridge	SO	13	B1
Prittlewell	ER	33	C1		Roby	LM	45	A2
Prudhoe	ER	67	C2		Rochdale	LM	55	C1
Pulborough	SO	11	C2		Roche	WR	1	B2
Purfleet	ER	32	C2		Rochester	SO	13	A1
Purley	SO	17	C2		Rochford	ER	33	C1
Purley Oaks	SO	17	C2		Rock Ferry	LM	53	C1
Putney	SO	20	C2		Roding Valley	LT	24	C2
Putney Bridge	LT	21	C1		Rogart	SC	81	B2
Pwllheli	LM	43	C2		Rolleston	LM	48	B1
Quaker's Yard	WR	27	C2		Rolvenden	KS	13	B1
Queenborough	SO	33	C1		Roman Bridge	LM	44	B1
Queen's Park (Glasgow)	SC	76	C1		Romford	ER	32	C2
Queen's Park (London)	LM/LT	21	B1		Romiley	LM	52	C2
Queen's Road, Battersea	SO	21	C1		Romsey	SO	10	C1
Queensbury	LT	31	C2		Roose	LM	54	A1
Queensway	LT	21	B1		Ropley	MH	10	B2
Quintrel Downs	WR	1	B2		Rose Grove	LM	55	B1
Quorn & Woodhouse	ML	38	A2		Rose Hill (Marple)	LM	52	C2
Radcliffe (Greater Manchester)	LM	55	C1		Rossall	BF	54	B1
Radcliffe (Notts)	LM	47	C2		Rosyth	SC	73	A1
Radipole	SO	5	A1		Rosyth Dockyard*	SC	73	A1
Radlett	LM	31	B2		Rotherham	ER	47	A1
Radley	WR	30	B2		Rotherhithe	LT	22	C1
Radyr	WR	28	C1		Rothley	ML	38	A2
Rainford	LM	54	C2		Rowland's Castle	SO	11	C1
Rainham (Essex)	ER	32	C2		Rowley Regis	LM	37	B2
Rainham (Kent)	SO	13	A1		Rowntree Halt*	ER	56	C2
Rainhill	LM	45	A2		Royal Oak	LT	21	B1
Ramsey	ME	59	B2		Roy Bridge	SC	78	A1
Ramsgate	SO	14	A1		Roydon	ER	32	B1
Rannoch	SC	78	B1		Royston	ER	32	A1
Rauceby	ER	48	C2		Royton Junction	LM	52	A2
Ravenglass	LM/RE	59	C2		Ruabon	LM	45	C1
Ravensbourne	SO	18	A1		Rufford	LM	54	C2
Ravenscourt Park	LT	20	C2		Rugby	LM	38	B2
Ravensthorpe	ER	56	C1		Rugeley	LM	37	A2
Rawcliffe	ER	57	B1		Ruislip	LT	19	A2
Rayleigh	ER	33	C1		Ruislip Gardens	LT	19	A2
Rayners Lane	LT	19	A2		Ruislip Manor	LT	19	A2
Raynes Park	SO	16	B2		Runcorn	LM	45	A2
Reading	WR	31	C1		Ruskington	ER	48	B2
Reading West	WR	31	C1		Russell Square	LT	21	B2
Rectory Road	ER	21	A2		Ruswarp	ER	63	B1
Redbridge (Greater London)	LT	22	A2		Rutherglen	SC	76	C1
Redbridge (Herts)	SO	10	C1		Ryde Esplanade	SO	6	A2
Redcar Central	ER	62	A2		Ryde Pier Head	SO	6	A2
Redcar East	ER	62	A2		Ryde St. John's Road	SO	6	A2
Reddish North	LM	52	B1		Rye	SO	13	C1
Reddish South	LM	52	C1		Rye House	ER	32	B1

St. Albans Abbey	LM	31	B2	Selling	SO	13	A2
St. Albans City	LM	31	B2	Selly Oak	LM	37	B2
St. Andrews Road	WR	28	C2	Selsdon	SO	17	C2
St. Annes-on-the-Sea	LM	54	B1	Settle	LM	55	A1
St. Austell	WR	1	B2	Seven Kings	ER	32	C1
St. Bees	LM	59	B2	Sevenoaks	SO	12	A2
St. Botolphs	ER	33	A2	Seven Sisters	ER/LT	21	A2
St. Budeaux (Ferry Road)	WR	2	B2	Severn Beach	WR	28	C2
St. Budeaux (Victoria Road)	WR	2	B2	Severn Tunnel Junction	WR	28	C2
St. Columb Road	WR	1	B2	Shadwell	LT	22	B1
St. Denys	SO	10	C1	Shalford	SO	11	B2
St. Enoch	GG	76	B1	Shanklin	SO	6	A2
St. Erth	WR	1	A1	Shaw	LM	55	C2
St. George's Cross	GG	76	B1	Shawford	SO	10	B2
St. Germans	WR	2	B2	Shawlands	SC	75	C2
St. Helens Junction	LM	45	A2	Sheerness-on-Sea	SO	33	C1
St. Helens Shaw Street	LM	45	A2	Sheffield	ER	47	A1
St. Helier	SO	17	B1	Sheffield Park	BL	12	B1
St. Ives	WR	1	A1	Shelford	ER	40	C1
St. James' Park	WR	3	A2	Shenfield	ER	32	C2
St. James' Street	ER	22	A1	Shenstone	LM	37	A2
St. John's Wood	LT	21	B1	Shepherd's Bush	LT	20	B2
St. Johns	SO	22	C1	Shepherd's Well	SO	14	A1
St. Keyne	WR	2	B1	Shepley	ER	56	C1
St. Leonards Warrior Square	SO	13	C1	Shepperton	SO	15	B1
St. Margaret's (Herts)	ER	32	B1	Shepreth	ER	40	C1
St. Margaret's (Surrey)	SO	16	A1	Sherborne	WR	8	C2
St. Mary's Bay	RH	13	B2	Sheringham	ER/NN	50	C1
St. Mary Cray	SO	12	A1	Shettleston	SC	76	B2
St. Michaels	LM	53	C2	Shields Road	GG	76	B1
St. Neots	ER	39	C2	Shifnal	LM	37	A1
St. Pancras	LM	21	B2	Shildon	ER	62	A1
St. Paul's	LT	21	B2	Shiplake	WR	31	C1
Sale	LM	51	C2	Shipley	ER	56	B1
Salford	LM	51	B2	Shippea Hill	ER	40	B2
Salfords	SO	12	B1	Shipton	WR	30	B1
Salhouse	ER	42	A1	Shirehampton	WR	28	C2
Salisbury	SO	9	B2	Shireoaks	ER	47	A2
Saltash	WR	2	B2	Shirley	LM	37	B2
Saltburn	ER	62	A2	Shoeburyness	ER	33	C1
Saltcoats	SC	71	C1	Sholing	SO	10	C2
Saltmarshe	ER	57	B1	Shoreditch	LT	21	B2
Salwick	LM	54	B2	Shoreham (Kent)	SO	12	A2
Sandbach	LM	46	B1	Shoreham-by-Sea	SO	12	C1
Sanderstead	SO	17	C2	Shortlands	SO	18	B1
Sandhills	LM	53	B1	Shotton	LM	45	B1
Sandhurst	SO	11	A1	Shrewsbury	LM	36	A2
Sandling for Hythe	SO	13	B2	Sidcup	SO	32	C1
Sandown	SO	6	A2	Silecroft	LM	60	C1
Sandplace	WR	2	B1	Silverdale	LM	60	C2
Sandwich	SO	14	A1	Silver Street	ER	23	C2
Sandy	ER	39	C2	Silvertown	ER	22	B2
Sankey for Penketh	LM	45	A2	Sinfin Central	LM	47	C1
Saundersfoot	WR	26	B1	Sinfin North	LM	47	C1
Saunderton	LM	31	C1	Singer	SC	75	A1
Sawbridgeworth	ER	32	B2	Sittingbourne	SO/SK	13	A1
Saxilby	ER	48	A1	Skegness	ER	49	B2
Saxmundham	ER	42	C1	Skelmanthorpe	ER	56	C1
Scarborough	ER	63	C2	Skipton	LM	55	A2
Scotscalder	SC	82	A1	Slade Green	SO	32	C2
Scotstounhill	SC	75	B2	Slateford	SC	73	A1
Scunthorpe	ER	57	C1	Sleaford	ER	48	C2
Seaburn	ER	70	C2	Sleights	ER	63	B1
Seaford	SO	12	C2	Sloane Square	LT	21	C1
Seaforth & Litherland	LM	53	A1	Slough	WR	31	C2
Seaham	ER	68	C2	Small Heath	LM	38	B2
Seamer	ER	63	C2	Smethwick Rolfe Street	LM	37	B2
Sea Mills	WR	28	C2	Smethwick West	LM	37	B2
Seascale	LM	59	B2	Smitham	SO	12	A1
Seaton	ST	4	A1	Snaefell	ME	59	C1
Seaton Carew	ER	62	A2	Snaith	ER	56	B2
Seer Green	LM	31	C2	Snaresbrook	LT	22	A2
Selby	ER	56	B2	Snodland	SO	12	A2
Selhurst	SO	17	B2	Snowdon Summit	SM	43	B2
Sellafield	LM	59	B2	Snowdown & Nonington	SO	13	A2

Sole Street	SO	12	A2	Stewarton	SC	71	B2
Solihull	LM	37	B2	Stirling	SC	78	C2
Somerleyton	ER	42	B1	Stockport	LM	52	C1
South Acton	LM	20	C2	Stocksfield	ER	67	C2
Southall	WR	19	C2	Stocksmoor	ER	56	C1
Southampton	SO	10	C1	Stockton	ER	62	B2
Southampton Airport	SO	10	C2	Stockwell	LT	21	C2
Southampton Docks	SO	10	C1	Stoke-on-Trent	LM	46	C1
South Bank	ER	62	A2	Stoke Mandeville	LM	31	B1
South Beach	SC	71	C1	Stoke Newington	ER	21	A2
South Bermondsey	SO	22	C1	Stone	LM	46	C1
Southbourne	SO	11	C1	Stonebridge Park	LM/LT	20	B2
Southbury	ER	24	B1	Stone Crossing	SO	32	C2
South Cape	ME	59	C2	Stonegate	SO	12	B2
South Croydon	SO	17	C2	Stonehaven	SC	79	A2
South Ealing	LT	20	C1	Stonehouse	WR	28	B1
Southease & Rodmell	SO	12	C1	Stoneleigh	SO	16	C2
South Elmsall	ER	56	C2	Stourbridge Junction	LM	37	B2
Southend Central	ER	33	C1	Stourbridge Town	LM	37	B1
Southend East	ER	33	C1	Stowmarket	ER	41	C2
Southend Victoria	ER	33	C1	Stranraer Harbour	SC	64	C1
Southfields	LT	17	A1	Stratford	ER/LT	22	B1
Southgate	LT	23	C2	Stratford-upon-Avon	LM	38	C1
South Gosforth	ER	69	A2	Strathcarron	SC	80	C2
South Greenford	WR	20	B1	Strawberry Hill	SO	16	A1
South Hampstead	LM	21	B1	Streatham	SO	17	A2
South Harrow	LT	20	A1	Streatham Common	SO	17	A2
South Kensington	LT	21	C1	Streatham Hill	SO	17	A2
South Kenton	LM/LT	20	A1	Stretford	LM	51	C2
South Merton	SO	17	B1	Strines	LM	46	A1
South Milford	ER	56	A2	Stromeferry	SC	80	C2
Southminster	ER	33	B1	Strood	SO	13	A1
Southport	LM	54	C1	Stroud	WR	29	B1
South Ruislip	LM/LT	19	A2	Sturry	SO	13	A2
South Shields	ER	70	B2	Styal	LM	46	A1
South Tottenham	ER	21	A2	Sudbury	ER	33	A1
Southwick	SO	12	C1	Sudbury & Harrow Road	LM	20	A1
South Wimbledon	LT	17	A1	Sudbury Hill	LT	20	A1
South Woodford	LT	24	C2	Sudbury Hill, Harrow	LM	20	A1
Sowerby Bridge	ER	55	B2	Sudbury Town	LT	20	A1
Spalding	ER	49	C1	Sunbury	SO	15	A2
Spean Bridge	SC	78	A1	Sunderland	ER	70	C2
Spital	LM	53	C1	Sundridge Park	SO	18	A2
Spondon	LM	47	C1	Sunningdale	SO	11	A1
Spooner Row	ER	41	B2	Sunnymeads	SO	31	C2
Springburn	SC	76	B1	Surbiton	SO	16	B1
Springfield	SC	79	C1	Surrey Docks	LT	22	C1
Spring Road	LM	37	B2	Sutton	SO	17	C1
Squires Gate	LM	54	B1	Sutton Coldfield	LM	37	B2
Stafford	LM	46	C2	Sutton Common	SO	17	B1
Staines	SO	15	A1	Swale	SO	13	A1
Stainforth & Hatfield	ER	56	C2	Swanley	SO	12	A2
Stallingborough	ER	58	C1	Swanscombe	SO	32	C2
Stalybridge	LM	52	B2	Swansea	WR	27	C1
Stamford	ER	39	A2	Swathling	SO	10	C1
Stamford Brook	LT	20	C2	Sway	SO	10	C1
Stamford Hill	ER	21	A2	Swinderby	ER	48	B1
Stanford-le-Hope	ER	32	C2	Swindon	WR	29	C2
Stanlow & Thornton	LM	45	A2	Swineshead	ER	49	C1
Stanmore	LT	31	C2	Swinton	LM	51	A2
Stansted	ER	32	A2	Swiss Cottage	LT	21	B1
Staplehurst	SO	13	B1	Sydenham	SO	18	A1
Stapleton Road	WR	8	A2	Sydenham Hill	SO	17	A2
Starbeck	ER	56	A1	Sylfaen	WL	36	A1
Starcross	WR	3	A2	Syon Lane	SO	20	C1
Starr Gate	BF	54	B1	Tackley	WR	30	B2
Staveley	LM	60	B2	Tadworth	SO	12	A1
Staverton Bridge	DV	3	B1	Taffs Well	WR	28	C1
Stechford	LM	37	B2	Tain	SC	81	B2
Stepney East	ER	22	B1	Talbot Square	BF	54	B1
Stepney Green	LT	22	B1	Talwrn Bach	LM	43	C2
Stevenage	ER	32	A1	Talybont	LM	33	A2
Stevenston	SC	71	C1	Tal-y-Cafn	LM	44	A1
Stewartby	LM	31	A2	Tamworth	LM	37	A1

Station	Region	Page	Grid
Tan-y-Bwlch	FR	44	C1
Tan-y-Grisiau	FR	44	C1
Taplow	WR	31	C1
Tattenham Corner	SO	12	A1
Taunton	WR	8	B1
Taynuilt	SC	77	B2
Teddington	SO	16	A1
Tees-side Airport	ER	62	B1
Teignmouth	WR	3	B2
Telford Central (Proposed)	LM	37	A1
Temple	LT	21	B2
Tenby	WR	26	B1
Tenterden	KS	13	B1
Teynham	SO	13	A1
Thames Ditton	SO	16	B1
Thatcham	WR	10	A2
Thatto Heath	LM	45	A2
Theale	WR	10	A2
The Dell	WR	1	C1
The Lakes	LM	37	B2
Theobalds Grove	ER	24	A1
The Pilot Halt	RH	13	C2
Thetford	ER	41	B1
Theydon Bois	LT	32	B1
Thirsk	ER	62	C2
Thornaby	ER	62	B2
Thorne North	ER	57	C1
Thorne South	ER	57	C1
Thornford	WR	8	C2
Thornliebank	SC	75	C2
Thornton Abbey	ER	57	C2
Thornton Gate	BF	54	B1
Thorntonhall	SC	72	B1
Thornton Heath	SO	17	B2
Thorpe Bay	ER	33	C1
Thorpe Culvert	ER	49	B2
Thorpe-le-Soken	ER	33	B2
Three Bridges	SO	12	B1
Three Oaks & Guestling	SO	13	C1
Thurgarten	LM	48	B1
Thurso	SC	82	A1
Thurston	ER	41	C1
Tilbury Riverside	ER	32	C2
Tilbury Town	ER	32	C2
Tile Hill	LM	38	B1
Tilehurst	WR	30	C2
Timperley	LM	51	C2
Tipton	LM	37	B2
Tir Phil	WR	28	B1
Tisbury	WR	9	B2
Tiverton Junction	WR	7	C2
Todmorden	LM	55	B2
Tolworth	SO	16	B2
Tonbridge	SO	12	B2
Tonfanau	LM	33	A2
Tonypandy	WR	27	C2
Tooting	SO	17	A1
Tooting Bec	LT	17	A1
Tooting Broadway	LT	17	A1
Topsham	WR	3	A2
Torquay	WR	3	B2
Torre	WR	3	B2
Totnes	WR	3	B1
Totnes Riverside	DV	3	B1
Tottenham Court Road	LT	21	B2
Tottenham Hale	ER/LT	21	A2
Totteridge & Whetstone	LT	23	C1
Totton	SO	10	C1
Tower	BF	54	B1
Tower Hill	LT	21	B2
Town Green	LM	54	C2
Trafford Park	LM	51	B2
Treforest	WR	27	C2
Treforest Estate	WR	27	C2
Trehafod	WR	27	C2
Treherbert	WR	27	B2
Treorchy	WR	27	C2
Trimley	ER	34	A1
Tring	LM	31	B1
Troedyrhiw	WR	27	B2
Troon	SC	71	C2
Trowbridge	WR	9	A1
Truro	WR	1	C2
Tufnell Park	LT	21	A1
Tulloch	SC	78	A1
Tulse Hill	SO	17	A2
Tunbridge Wells Central	SO	12	B2
Tunbridge Wells West	SO	12	B2
Turkey Street	ER	24	B1
Turnham Green	LT	20	C2
Turnpike Lane	LT	23	C2
Twickenham	SO	16	A1
Twyford	WR	31	C1
Ty Croes	LM	43	A1
Tygwyn	LM	43	C2
Tyndrum Lower	SC	78	B1
Tyndrum Upper	SC	78	B1
Tyne Dock	ER	70	B2
Tynemouth	ER	70	A2
Tyseley	LM	37	B2
Tywyn	LM	34	A2
Tywyn Pendre	TL	34	A2
Tywyn Wharf	TL	34	A2
Uckfield	SO	12	C2
Uddingston	SC	76	C2
Ulceby	ER	57	C2
Ulleskelf	ER	56	B2
Ulverston	LM	60	C1
Umberleigh	WR	7	C1
University (Birmingham)	LM	37	B2
Upholland	LM	54	C2
Upminster	ER/LT	32	C2
Upminster Bridge	LT	32	C2
Upney	LT	32	C1
Upper Halliford	SO	15	B2
Upper Holloway	LM	21	A2
Upper Warlingham	SO	12	A1
Upton	LM	45	A1
Upton-by-Chester	LM	45	B2
Upton Park	LT	22	B2
Upwey & Broadway	SO	5	A1
Urmston	LM	51	C1
Uttoxeter	LM	46	C2
Uxbridge	LT	19	B1
Vauxhall	SO/LT	21	C2
Victoria	SO/LT	21	C1
Virginia Water	SO	11	A2
Waddon	SO	17	C2
Waddon Marsh	SO	17	B2
Wadhurst	SO	12	B2
Wadsley Bridge*	ER	47	A1
Wainfleet	ER	49	B2
Wakefield Kirkgate	ER	56	C1
Wakefield Westgate	ER	56	C1
Walkden	LM	51	A1
Walker Gate	ER	69	B2
Wallasey Grove Road	LM	53	B1
Wallasey Village	LM	53	B1
Wallington	SO	17	C1
Wallsend	ER	70	B1
Walmer	SO	14	A1
Walsall	LM	37	A2
Waltham Cross	ER	24	A1
Walthamstow Central	ER/LT	22	A1
Walthamstow Queen's Road	ER	22	A1
Walton (Merseyside)	LM	53	A2
Walton-on-Naze	ER	33	B2
Walton-on-Thames	SO	15	C2
Wanborough	SO	11	A1
Wansford	NV	39	A2

Station	Region	No.	Grid
Wandsworth Common	SO	17	A1
Wandsworth Road	SO	21	C2
Wandsworth Town	SO	21	C1
Wanstead	LT	22	A2
Wanstead Park	ER	22	A2
Wapping	LT	22	B1
Warblington	SO	11	C1
Ware	ER	32	B1
Wareham	SO	5	A2
Wargrave	WR	31	C1
Warminster	SO	9	B1
Warnham	SO	11	B2
Warrenby*	ER	62	A2
Warren Street	LT	21	B2
Warrington Bank Quay	LM	45	A2
Warrington Central	LM	45	A2
Warwick	LM	38	C1
Warwick Avenue	LT	21	B1
Warwick Road	LM	51	B2
Washford Halt	WS	7	B2
Watchet	WS	7	B2
Wateringbury	SO	12	A2
Waterloo (London)	SO/LT	21	B2
Waterloo (Merseyside)	LM	53	A1
Water Orton	LM	38	B1
Watford	LT	31	C2
Watford High Street	LM/LT	31	C2
Watford Junction	LM/LT	31	C2
Watford North	LM	31	B2
Watford West	LM	31	C2
Wedgwood	LM	46	C1
Weeley	ER	33	B2
Weeton	ER	56	A1
Welling	SO	32	C1
Wellingborough	LM	39	C1
Wellington	LM	37	A1
Wellworthy Ampress Works Halt*	SO	6	A1
Welshpool	LM	36	A1
Welwyn Garden City	ER	32	B1
Welwyn North	ER	32	B1
Wem	LM	45	C2
Wembley Central	LM/LT	20	A1
Wembley Hill	LM	20	A2
Wembley Park	LT	20	A2
Wemyss Bay	SC	71	A1
Wendover	LM	31	B1
Wennington	LM	54	A2
West Acton	LT	20	B1
West Allerton	LM	53	C2
Westbourne Park	WR/LT	21	B1
West Brompton	LT	21	C1
Westbury	WR	9	A1
West Byfleet	SO	15	C1
West Calder	SC	72	B2
Westcliff	ER	33	C1
Westcombe	SO	22	C2
West Croydon	SO	17	B2
West Drayton	WR	19	B1
West Dulwich	SO	17	A2
West Ealing	WR	20	B1
Westenhanger	SO	13	B2
Westerfield	ER	33	A2
Westerton	SC	75	A2
West Finchley	LT	23	C1
Westgate-on-Sea	SO	14	A1
West Ham	LT	22	B1
West Hampstead	LM/LT	21	A1
West Harrow	LT	20	A1
West Horndon	ER	32	C2
Westhoughton	LM	55	C1
West Jesmond	ER	69	B2
West Kensington	LT	21	C1
West Kilbride	SC	71	B1
West Kirkby	LM	45	A1
West Malling	SO	12	A2
Westminster	LT	21	B2
West Monkseaton	ER	70	A1
West Norwood	SO	17	A2
Weston Milton	WR	8	A1
Weston-super-Mare	WR	8	A1
West Ruislip	LM/LT	19	A2
West Runton	ER	50	C1
West St. Leonards	SO	13	C1
West Street	GG	76	B1
West Sutton	SO	17	C1
West Wickham	SO	18	B1
West Worthing	SO	11	C2
Weybourne	NN	50	C1
Weybridge	SO	15	C1
Weymouth	SO	5	A1
Weymouth Quay	SO	5	A1
Whaley Bridge	LM	46	A2
Whatstandwell	LM	47	B1
Whimple	WR	3	A2
Whitby	ER	63	B1
Whitchurch (Hants)	SO	10	A2
Whitchurch (Salop)	LM	45	C2
Whitchurch (South Glam)	WR	28	C1
Whitechapel	LT	22	B1
White City	LT	20	B2
Whitecraigs	SC	75	C2
Whitefield	LM	51	A2
White Hart Lane	ER	23	C2
Whitehaven	LM	59	B2
White Notley	ER	33	B1
Whitland	WR	26	B1
Whitley Bay	ER	70	A2
Whitley Bridge	ER	56	B2
Whitlock's End	LM	37	B2
Whitstable & Tankerton	SO	13	A2
Whittlesea	ER	40	B1
Whittlesford	ER	32	A2
Whitton	SO	16	A1
Whyteleafe	SO	12	A1
Whyteleafe South	SO	12	A1
Wick	SC	82	A1
Wickford	ER	33	C1
Wickham Market	ER	42	C1
Widdrington	ER	68	B1
Widnes	LM	45	A2
Widney Manor	LM	37	B2
Wigan North Western	LM	54	C2
Wigan Wallgate	LM	54	C2
Wigton	LM	66	C1
Willesden Green	LT	20	A2
Willesden Junction	LM/LT	20	B2
Williamwood	SC	75	C2
Williton	WS	7	B2
Wilmcote	LM	38	C1
Wilmslow	LM	46	A1
Wilnecote	LM	38	A1
Wimbledon	SO/LT	17	A1
Wimbledon Chase	SO	17	B1
Winchelsea	SO	13	C1
Winchester	SO	10	B2
Winchfield	SO	11	A1
Winchmore Hill	ER	23	C2
Windermere	LM	60	B2
Windsor & Eton Central	WR	31	C2
Windsor & Eton Riverside	SO	31	C2
Winnersh	SO	11	A1
Winsford	LM	46	B1
Wishaw	SC	72	B1
Witham	ER	33	B1
Witley	SO	11	B2
Wittersham Road	KS	13	B1
Witton	LM	37	B2
Wivelsfield	SO	12	C1
Wivenhoe	ER	33	B2

Woburn Sands	LM	31	A1		Worksop	ER	47	A2
Woking	SO	11	A2		Worplesden	SO	11	A2
Wokingham	SO	11	A1		Worstead	ER	50	C2
Woldingham	SO	12	A1		Worthing	SO	11	C2
Wolverhampton	LM	37	A2		Wrabness	ER	33	A2
Wolverton	LM	31	A1		Wraysbury	SO	31	C2
Wombwell	ER	56	C1		Wrenbury	LM	45	B2
Woodbridge	ER	42	C1		Wressle	ER	57	B1
Wood End	LM	37	C2		Wrexham Central	LM	45	B1
Woodford	LT	24	C2		Wrexham Exchange	LM	45	B1
Woodgrange Park	ER	22	A2		Wrexham General	LM	45	B1
Wood Green	ER/LT	23	C2		Wroxham	ER	42	A1
Woodhall	SC	71	A2		Wye	SO	13	A2
Woodham Ferrers	ER	33	B1		Wylam	ER	67	C2
Woodhouse	ER	47	C1		Wylde Green	LM	37	B2
Woodlands Road	LM	52	A1		Wymondham	ER	41	A2
Woodlesford	ER	56	B1		Wythall	LM	37	B2
Woodmansterne	SO	12	A1		Yalding	SO	12	A2
Woodside	SO	18	B1		Yardley Wood	LM	37	B2
Woodside Park	LT	23	C1		Yarmouth	ER	42	A2
Wood Street	ER	22	A1		Yatton	WR	8	A2
Wool	SO	5	A1		Yeoford	WR	3	A1
Woolston	SO	10	C2		Yeovil Junction	WR	8	C2
Woolwich Arsenal	SO	22	C2		Yeovil Pen Mill	WR	8	C2
Woolwich Dockyard	SO	22	C2		Yetminster	WR	8	C2
Wootton Wawen	LM	37	C2		Yoker	SC	75	A2
Worcester Foregate Street	WR	37	C1		York	ER	56	A2
Worcester Park	SO	16	B2		Yorton	LM	45	C2
Worcester Shrub Hill	WR	37	C1		Ystrad Mynach	WR	28	C1
Workington	LM	59	A2		Ystrad Rhonnda	WR	27	C2

REGION & RAILWAY CODES

BA   Bala Lake Railway
BF   Blackpool & Fleetwood Tramway
BL   Bluebell Railway
DV   Dart Valley Railway
ER   British Rail — Eastern
FB   Fairbourne Railway
FR   Festiniog Railway
GG   Greater Glasgow P.T.E.
GO   Great Orme Tramway
IW   Isle of Wight Railway
KW   Keighley & Worth Valley Railway
KS   Kent & East Sussex Railway
LH   Lakeside & Haverthwaite Railway
LL   Llanberis Lake Railway
LM   British Rail — London Midland
LT   London Transport
ME   Manx Electric Railway
MH   Mid-Hants Railway
ML   Main Line Steam Trust
MS   Manx Steam Railway
NN   North Norfolk Railway
NV   Nene Valley Railway
NY   North Yorkshire Moors Railway
RE   Ravenglass & Eskdale Railway
RH   Romney, Hythe & Dymchurch Railway
SC   British Rail — Scottish
SK   Sittingbourne and Kemsley Railway
SM   Snowdon Mountain Railway
SO   British Rail — Southern
ST   Strathspey Railway
SV   Severn Valley Railway
TD   Torbay and Dartmouth Railway
TL   Talyllyn Railway
WL   Welshpool & Llanfair Railway
WR   British Rail — Western
WS   West Somerset Railway

INDEX TO BRITISH RAIL ENGINEERING LTD. WORKS

INDEX TO BRITISH RAIL DEPOTS AND STABLING POINTS

(Total 146)

INDEX TO FREIGHT TERMINALS AND YARDS

Clyde's Mill P.S.	76	C2		Eastgate	61	A2
Clydebridge Steelwks	76	C1		East Leake	47	C2
Clydeport FLT	71	A1		Eastriggs	66	C1
Coalville	38	A1		Ebbw Vale Steelwks	28	B1
Cockenzie P.S.	73	A2		Edwalton	47	C2
Coed Bach Coll.	26	B2		Eggborough P.S.	56	B2
Coed Ely Coll.	27	C2		Egremont	59	B2
Coity Goods, Bridgend	27	C2		Ellington Coll.	68	B1
Colnbrook	19	C1		Elmham	41	A1
Coltness	72	B1		Elmley Lovett	37	C1
Colton Wood Coll.	56	C1		Elsecar Main Coll.	56	C1
Colwick Steelwks.	47	C2		Emley Moor Coll.	56	C1
Comrie Coll. (Saline)	72	A2		Erskine	75	A1
Conington South	39	B2		Eskmeals	59	B2
Connah's Quay P.S.	45	B1		Etherley	62	A1
Corby	39	B1		Evanton	81	C2
Corringham Oil Ref.	32	C2		Fakenham	50	C1
Curton Wood Coll.	56	C1		Fallin Coll.	78	C2
Coryton Oil Ref.	33	C1		Far Cotton	39	C1
Cotgrave Coll.	47	C2		Farnley	56	B1
Coton Hill Yard (Shrewsbury)	36	A2		Faslane	71	A1
Cottam P.S.	48	A1		Fawcett Street (Sunderland)	70	C2
Cowie	72	A2		Fawley	10	C2
Coxhoe Quarry	62	A1		Felixstowe Docks & FLT	34	A1
Craig-y-Nos Quarry HST	27	B1		Ferguslie	75	B1
Craigentinny C.S. & HST Depot	73	A1		Ferrybridge P.S.	56	B2
CRAIGINCHES YARD, Aberdeen	79	A2		Ferryhill (Aberdeen)	79	A2
Craigneuk Steelwks	72	B1		Ferry Road (Grangetown)	28	C1
Cranmore	9	B1		Fiddlers Ferry P.S.	45	A2
Cransley	39	B1		Fishburn Cooking Plant	62	A1
Crawley New Yard (P.W.)	12	B1		Fleetwood P.S.	54	A1
Creekmouth P.S.	32	C2		Fletton	39	A2
Creigiau Quarry	27	C2		Flixborough	57	C1
Crombie	72	A2		Florence Coll.	46	C2
Cronton Coll.	45	A2		Foley Park	37	B1
Croxley Mill	31	C2		Follingsby Coll.	70	C1
Culloden Moor	81	C2		Follingsby FLT	70	C1
Curzon Street (Birmingham)	38	B2		Folly Lane	45	A2
Cwm Bargoed Coll.	27	B2		Forfar	79	B1
Cwm Coll.	27	C2		Fort Dunlop	37	B2
Cwmmawr Coll.	26	B2		Forth Goods (Newcastle)	69	B2
Cynheidre Coll.	26	B2		Fowey	2	B1
Dailly Coll.	64	A1		Frances Coll. (Dysart)	79	C1
Darfield Coll.	56	C1		Fraserburgh	82	C2
Dawdon Coll.	68	C2		Fremington Quay	6	B2
Daw Mill Coll. (Whiteacre)	38	B1		Frickley Coll.	56	C2
Dean Hill	10	B1		Frodingham Steelwks (Scunthorpe)	57	C1
Denby Coll.	47	C1		Frosterley Quarry	61	A2
Deptford	70	C2		Fryston Coll.	56	B2
Dereham	41	A1		Furzebrook	5	A2
Derwent Haugh Coking Plant	69	B1		Galley Hill	13	C1
Desford Coll.	38	A2		Garston Docks & FLT	53	C2
Dewsnap Sdgs.	52	B2		Gartherrie FLT	72	B1
Didcot P.S.	30	C2		Garw Coll.	27	C2
Dinnington Coll.	47	A2		Gatewen Coll.	45	B1
Dinton	9	B2		Gedling Coll.	47	C2
Dodworth Coll.	56	C1		General Terminus	76	B1
Donisthorpe Coll.	38	A1		Glapwell Coll.	47	B2
Donnington	37	A1		Glascoed	28	B1
Dowlais	27	B2		Glass Houghton Coll.	56	B2
Drakelow P.S.	38	A1		Glenrothes	79	C1
Drax P.S.	56	B2		Glodwick Road (Oldham)	52	A2
Drayton Gravel Term.	11	C1		Golbourne Coll.	54	C2
DRINGHOUSES YARD, York	56	A2		Goldthorpe Coll.	56	C2
Drinnick Mill	1	B2		Gorseinon	26	B2
Dudley FLT	37	B2		Gosford Green	38	B1
Dudley Hill	56	B1		Graig Merthyr Coll.	27	B1
Dufftown	82	C1		Grain Oil Ref	33	C1
Dunnington	56	A2		Grangemouth	72	A2
Dunstable	31	A2		Granton	73	A1
Dunston P.S.	69	B1		Granville Coll.	37	A1
Dunston Straithes	69	B2		Great Mountain Coll.	26	B2
Dyserth	44	A2		Griffen	71	B2
Earley P.S.	31	C1		Grimethorpe Coll.	56	C2
Easington Coll.	62	A2		Gushetfaulds FLT	76	B1
East Caudledown	1	B2		Gwauncaegurwen Coll.	27	B1

Location	No.	Code	Location	No.	Code
Hafodyrynys Coll.	28	B1	Lawley Street (Birmingham)	38	B2
Haig Coll.	59	B2	Layerthorpe	56	A2
Halliwell	55	C1	Lea Hall Coll.	37	A2
Hallside Steelwks	76	C2	Ledston Luck Coll.	56	B2
Hams Hall P.S.	38	B1	Lenton	42	C1
Hamworthy Goods	5	A2	Leith	73	A1
Harbury Cem. Wks	38	C1	Lenwade	41	A2
Hardingstone P.S.	39	C1	Leven P.S.	79	C1
Harlaxton	48	C1	Leyburn	61	C2
Harrison's Limeworks (Shap)	60	B2	Linby Coll.	47	B2
Harworth Coll.	47	A2	Lindsey Oil Ref.	57	C2
Hatfield Coll.	56	C2	Linwood	75	B1
Hathersett	41	A2	Little Barford P.S.	39	C2
Havannah Coll.	69	A1	Littleton Coll.	37	A2
Haverton Hill	62	A2	Liverpool Road (Manchester)	51	B2
Hawkesbury P.S.	38	B1	Liversedge	56	B1
Hawkhead	75	B1	Llandarcy Oil Ref	27	C1
Hawthorn Coking Works	68	C2	Llanharan Coll.	27	C2
Haydock	54	C2	Llanwern Steelwks	28	C1
HEALEY MILLS YARD	56	C1	Llynfi P.S.	27	C2
Heathfield	3	A1	Longannet P.S.	72	A2
Heaton C.S.	69	B2	Longbridge	37	B2
Hemelite Works	31	B2	Long Marston	29	A2
Herbrandston	25	B2	Longsight FLT	52	B1
Herrington	68	C1	Longtowm	66	C2
Heysham	54	A2	Lostwithiel	2	B1
Hickleton Coll.	56	C2	Louth	49	A1
HITHER GREEN YARD	18	A2	Ludgershall	10	A1
Holborough	12	A2	Lydd	13	C2
Holditch Coll.	46	B1	Lynemouth	68	B1
Holmethorpe	12	A1	Machen Quarry	28	C1
Holyhead Breakwater	43	A1	Maerdy Coll.	27	B2
Holywell Coll.	70	A1	Maesteg Coll.	27	C1
Hope Cem. Wks	47	A1	Malago Vale C.S.	8	B2
Hope Street (Manchester)	51	A2	Maltby Coll.	47	A2
Hordon Coll.	62	A2	Mansfield Coll.	47	B2
Horrocksford Cem. Wks	55	B1	Mantle Lane, Coalville	38	A1
Horsehay & Dawley	37	A1	Manton Main Coll.	47	A1
Hotchley Hill	47	C2	Manuel	72	A2
Houghton-le-Spring	68	C1	Marchon Chem. Wks	59	B2
Hucknall Coll.	47	C2	Marchwood	10	C1
Hullavington	29	C2	MARGAM YARD	27	C1
Humber Oil Ref.	57	C2	Marine Coll.	28	B1
Humberstone Road (Leicester)	38	A2	Markham Coll. (Glam.)	28	B1
Huncoat P.S.	55	B1	Markham Coll. (Notts.)	47	B2
Hunterston	71	B1	Markham Main Coll. (S.Yorks)	56	C2
Hylton Coll.	70	C2	Marland	6	C2
Immingham Docks	57	C2	Marshgate (Doncaster)	56	C2
Ince	45	A2	Maud Jcn.	82	C2
Ireland Coll. (Staveley)	47	A2	Maudlands	45	B2
Irlam Steelworks	51	C1	Maxwelltown	65	B2
Ironbridge P.S.	37	A1	Mayfield Parcels (Manchester)	52	B1
Isebrook	39	B1	Meaford P.S.	46	C1
Ivybridge	3	B1	Measham Coll.	38	A1
JERSEY MARINE YARD	27	C1	Meeth	6	C2
Keadby P.S.	57	C1	Meldon	2	A2
Kellingley Coll.	56	B2	Meledor Mill	1	B2
Kennethmont	82	C1	Melksham	9	A1
Keresley Coll.	38	B1	Menstrie	76	C2
Ketton	39	A2	Merehead	9	B1
Killingholme Haven Oil Ref	57	C2	Merton Abbey	17	A1
Killoch Coll.	71	C2	Methil	79	C1
Kincardine P.S.	72	A2	Metro-Cammell	37	B2
KINGMOOR YARD	66	C2	Mickleover Test Centre	47	C1
Kingshill Coll.	72	B2	Middleton Towers	40	A2
Kingsnorth	33	C1	Middlewich	46	B1
Kinneil Coll.	72	A2	MILLERHILL YARD	73	A1
Kirk Sandall	56	C2	Millerston	76	B2
Kittybrewster	79	A2	Mill Lane (St. Helens)	54	C2
Lackenby	62	A2	Mill Pit Coll.	27	C1
Lady Windsor Coll.	27	C2	Millwall Docks	22	C1
Langwith Coll.	47	B2	Milton Inland Port	30	C2
Larkfield C.S.	76	B1	Mold	45	B1
Latimer Road	20	B2	Mond's Nickel Works	27	B1
Lavant	11	C1	Monk Bretton Coll.	56	C1

Monkton Coking Plant	70	B1		Portishead	28	C2
Monktonhall Coll.	73	A1		Portobello FLT	73	A1
Monmore Green	37	A2		Port Sunlight	53	C1
Moor Green Coll.	47	C2		Prestwick	69	A1
Moorswater	2	B1		Prince of Wales Coll.	56	B2
Moreton-on-Lugg	36	C2		Puriton	8	B1
Morris Cowley	30	B2		Purley	17	C2
Morriston	27	C1		Pye Hill Coll.	47	B2
MOSSEND YARD	72	B1		Quedgeley	29	B1
Mostyn	45	A1		Quidhampton	9	B2
Mountain Ash Coll.	27	B2		Radstock	9	A1
Mountfield Gypsum	12	C2		Radway Green	46	B1
Mountsorrel Quarry	38	A2		Raisby Quarry	62	A1
Nailstone Coll.	38	A1		Ratcliffe-on-Trent P.S.	47	C2
Nantgarw Coll.	27	C2		Ravenscraig Steelworks	72	B1
Nechells P.S.	37	B2		Rawden Coll.	38	A1
New Bilton Cement Wks	38	B2		Rawtenstall	55	C1
Newdigate Coll.	38	B1		Reading Central	11	A1
New Hucknall Coll.	47	B2		Red Bank C.S. (Manchester)	52	B1
Newland P.W. Depot	37	C1		Redcar Jetty	62	A2
Newmarket Coll.	56	B1		Redcar Jetty	62	A2
Newstead Coll.	47	B2		Redmire	61	C2
New Stubbin Coll.	47	A2		Renfrew Wharf	75	B2
Newtown Coll.	27	B2		Renishaw Park Coll.	47	A2
NEW YARD, Hull	57	B2		Resolven	27	B1
North Dock, Sandhills	53	B2		Rewley Road (Oxford)	30	B2
Northenden Cem. Wks	51	C2		Rhoose Cem. Wks	7	A2
North Gawber Coll.	56	C1		Ribbleton	54	B2
North Wilford P.S.	47	C2		Richborough P.S.	14	A1
Norton Jcn	37	A2		Ridham Docks	13	A1
Norwich (Victoria)	41	A2		Ripley	47	B1
Norwood Coking Plant	69	C2		RIPPLE LANE YARD	32	C2
Nostell Coll.	56	C1		Robeston	25	B2
Oakamoor	46	C2		Rockingham Coll.	56	C1
Oakdale Coll.	28	C1		Rogerstone P.S.	28	C1
Oldham Road (Manchester)	52	B1		Rose Heyworth Coll.	28	B1
Ollerton Coll.	47	B2		Rossington Coll.	56	C2
Onllwyn Coll.	27	B1		Rothwell Coll.	56	B1[
Orgreave Coll.	47	A2		Rowrah Quarry	59	B2
Oughtibridge	47	A1		Royston Coll.	56	C1
Oxley C.S.	37	A1		Ruddington	47	C2
Oxwellmains	74	A1		Rufford Coll.	47	B2
Padiham P.S.	55	B1		Rugeley P.S.	37	A2
Parkandillack	1	B2		Ryburgh	50	C1
Parkend	28	B2		Rye House P.S.	32	B1
Park Hill Coll.	56	B1		Rylstone Quarry	55	A2
Park Royal	20	B2		St Mary's Yard, Derby	47	C1
Parkside Coll.	45	A2		Saltend	57	B2
Peak Forest Quarry	46	A2		Saltley FLT	38	B2
Peckfield Coll.	56	B2		Santon	57	C2
Penallta Coll.	28	C1		Saville Coll.	56	B1
Penderyn Quarry	27	B2		Sculcoates P.S.	57	B2
Pengam FLT	28	C1		Seafield Coll.	73	A1
Pennyvenie Coll.	64	A2		Seaham Coll.	68	C2
Penrhiwceiber Coll.	27	C2		Seal Sands	62	A2
Pesnett	37	B1		Seaton Burn Coll.	68	A2
Pespool	62	A1		Seaton Snook	62	A2
Petrockstow	6	C2		SEVERN TUNNEL YARD	28	C2
Philadelphia	68	C1		Sharlston Coll.	56	C1
Piddington	39	B1		Sharpness	29	B1
Pig's Bay	33	C1		Sherwood Coll.	47	B2
Pinhoe	3	A2		Shieldhall	75	B2
Pitstone	31	B1		Shilbottle Coll.	68	A1
Pleasley Coll.	47	B2		Shirebrook Coll.	47	B2
Plumpherson	72	B2		Shireoaks Coll.	47	A2
Plymouth Friary	2	B2		Shotton Coll.	62	A1
Plymstock	2	B2		Shut End	37	B1
Point of Ayr Coll.	44	A2		Silverdale Coll.	46	B1
Polkemmet Coll. (Whitburn)	72	B2		Silverhill Coll.	47	B2
Ponsandane C.S. & HST Depot	1	A1		Silverwood Coll.	47	A2
Pontsmill	1	B2		Six Bells Coll.	28	B1
Poplar Docks	22	B1		Skelton Grange P.S.	56	B1
Port Clarence	62	A2		Skinningrove Ironworks	63	B1
Port Elphinstone	79	A2		Shalmstown	66	C2

Location	No.	Ref
Smeaton Coll.	73	A1
Snibston Coll.	38	A1
Soho Pool	37	B2
Southam Cem. Wks	38	C2
South Durham Steelwks	62	A2
Southerham Cem. Wks	12	C1
Southfleet	32	C2
South Hetton Coll.	68	C1
South Kirkby Coll.	56	C2
South Lambeth	20	C1
South Lynn	40	A2
SPEKE YARD	53	C2
Spondon P.S.	47	C1
Springwell Bank Foot	70	C1
Sproughton	33	A2
St Ives (Cambs)	40	C1
St Mary's Yard, Derby	47	C1
Stafford Coll. (Stoke)	46	C1
Staines West	15	A1
Stanfree	47	A2
Stanton	47	C2
Staveley Coll.	47	A2
Staveley Wks	47	A1
Staythorpe P.S.	48	B1
Steetley Coll.	47	A2
Stella North P.S.	69	B1
Stella South P.S.	69	B1
Stocksbridge Steelwks	56	C1
Stoneycombe Quarry	3	B1
Stourport P.S.	37	C1
Stourton Yard & FLT	56	B1
Stranraer Town	64	C1
Sutton-in-Ashfield	47	B2
Sutton Coll.	47	B2
Sutton Harbour	2	B2
Sutton Manor Coll.	45	A2
Swalwell Coll.	69	B1
Swansea East Dock	27	C1
Taff Merthyr Coll.	27	B2
Tallington	39	A2
Teesport	62	A2
TEES YARD	62	B2
TEMPLE MILLS YARD	22	A1
Teversal	47	B2
Thame	31	B1
Thames Haven Oil Ref	33	C1
Thoresby Coll.	47	B2
Thornhill P.S.	56	C1
Thornton	45	A2
Thorpe Marsh P.S.	56	C2
Thurcroft Coll.	47	A2
Tidenham Quarry	28	C2
Tilmanstone Coll.	14	A1
TINSLEY YARD	47	A1
Tintern Quarry	28	B2
Todd Lane Gas Works	54	B2
Topley Pike	46	A2
Torksey	48	A1
Torrington	6	C2
TOTON YARD	47	C2
Tower Coll.	27	B2
Trafford Park FLT	51	B2
Trawsfynydd	44	C1
Trecwn	25	A2
Treeton Coll.	47	A2
Trehaford Coll.	27	C2
Treharris Coll.	27	C2
Treviscoe	1	B2
Trostre Tinplate Wks	26	B2
Tunstead Quarry	46	A2
Tutbury	47	C1
Tuxford	48	B1
Twywell	39	B1
Tytherington	29	C1
Uskmouth P.S.	28	C1
Valley	43	A1
TYNE YARD	69	C2
Tytherington	29	C1
Uskmouth P.S.	28	C1
Valley	43	A1
Vane Tempest Coll.	68	C2
Velindre Tinplate Works	27	B1
Wadebridge	1	B2
Wallingford	30	C2
Walton Coll.	56	C1
Warcop	61	B1
Warsop Main Coll.	47	B2
WASHWOOD HEATH YARD	37	B2
Waterside	63	A2
Waterslack Quarry	60	C2
Waterston	25	B2
Watford Tip	31	C2
Wath Coll.	56	C2
WATH YARD	56	C2
Watton-at-Stone	32	B1
Wavetree Parcels	53	B2
Wednesfield	37	A2
Welbeck Coll.	47	B2
Wenford Bridge	2	A1
Wensum (Norwich)	41	A2
West Cannock Coll.	37	A2
West Cornforth Quarry	62	A1
Westcott	31	B1
Westfield Coll.	79	C1
West Ham P.S.	22	B1
Westhorpe Coll.	47	A2
Westoe Coll.	70	B2
West Thurrock P.S.	32	C2
Whatley Quarry	9	A1
Wheldale Coll.	56	B2
Whiteacre Coll.	38	B1
Whitebirk P.S.	56	B1
WHITEMOOR YARD	40	A1
Whittle Coll.	68	A1
Whitewell Coll.	47	A2
Widdrington Coll.	68	A1
WILLESDEN YARD	20	B2
Willington P.S.	47	C1
Wilton	62	A2
Windscale	59	B2
Windsor Coll.	27	C2
Windsor Street (Aston)	37	B2
Wintersett Coll.	56	C1
Wirksworth Quarry	47	B1
Wisbech	40	A1
Wissington	40	B2
Wolsingham	61	A2
Wolstanton Coll.	46	B1
Woodside	37	B2
Woolley Coll.	56	C1
Wootton Bassett Stone T.	29	C2
Worthington	47	C1
Yardley Chace (Piddington)	39	C1
Yaxley	39	B2
York Road (Doncaster)	56	C2
Yorkshire Main Coll.	56	C2